The Pebble in the Pond

The Pebble in the Pond

Entry Points and Conflicts That Can Cause Ripple Effects In Your Life

Lakeisha Stevenson

XULON PRESS

Xulon Press
2301 Lucien Way #415
Maitland, FL 32751
407.339.4217
www.xulonpress.com

Printed in the United States of America.

ISBN-13: 978-1-6305-0588-2

Lakeisha Stevenson has a depth of wisdom that has allowed her clients to win at overcoming the obstacles and challenges brought on by trauma. While a pebble in the pond is a small metaphor, it holds gigantic weight in the lives of those who are trapped and haunted by trauma. The only way for one to be free is to acknowledge that they were bound.

For some readers, this book will be an eye opener, for others it will serve as a confirmation. Nevertheless, if you follow and put into action the wisdom and revelation written on these pages, the generations to come after you will thank you greatly. Make a choice to be bigger and better by understanding the mandate for resolution.

Pastor Jesse Stevenson
Revive Church of Rockland, Nyack NY

TABLE OF CONTENTS

Foreword **ix**

Introduction- The IT **xiii**

1. You Have Purpose **1**

2. In Time **7**

3. Purpose Must Be Identified Early **13**

4. What Do You Possess? **21**

5. The IT of Trauma **27**

6. You Will Master IT **37**

7. The IT of Rejection **43**

8. Suppression **49**

9. When IT Makes You Mute **55**

10. The Struggle After The Wound **63**

11. What's Said Can Help To Frame You **73**

12. When IT Causes You To Fight **81**

13. The IT of Violation **91**

14. When IT Causes You To Fear **99**

15. When IT Causes You To Lose Confidence **105**

16. The IT of Grief **111**

17. Overcoming IT **125**

Work IT Out Questions **131**

References **157**

FOREWORD

In "The Pebble In The Pond" LaKeisha Stevenson has strategically outlined the process to purpose and the journey to successfully navigate IT! As you read, IT will transform the what, the why and the how, causing greater results, faster, increasing productivity levels personally & professionally.

LaKeisha shares clues and signs to avoid missteps and unintended collateral damage. This blueprint will empower readers that execute the plan to live on purpose through life's experiences. No matter the IT-impact you'll be positioned as a thought leader today and into the future!

Thank you LaKeisha for the model, live on purpose and respond to IT with actions of integrity, urgent execution and a commitment to help others win!

Dr. Stephen E. White
Author of "The 5 Essentials to Win"

This work is dedicated to Shenyetta K. Garner (my best friend and sister) and Melba Pompey (my maternal grandmother), two pillars of my life that I miss dearly; two of the most selfless and kind individuals that imprinted a lasting impression on me. They both possessed genuine characters to see others do well and offered their full support along the way. This two exemplified great courage and the ability to overcome many obstacles that were in their paths. "Ms. Sugar" or Shen, as we affectionately called Shenyetta, and "Ms. Bea," were the SWEETEST blessings that a girl could have. I feel assured that they believe in me, and I will continue to make them proud.

I honor God for allowing me to pen these words and share some once-vulnerable areas in my life. While writing this book, many times I thought I was finished writing, and then He led me to unveil even more, much more than I had planned initially. These pages promoted another level of healing and awareness for me, and my goal is that it will accomplish the same for you.

To my husband Jesse, for ensuring that I followed this through to completion and doing double duty with the little blessings, when I had to be in quiet spaces. Your encouragement and push for pro-gression and productivity is incomparable. I am elated that we do life together. I love you!

To our children, Jayla, Jesse II, Pearson, and Rai'Leigh: you are all joys to our lives, and we strive to show you how to excel and do well. We want you to be greater than we have been; you have all the goods. Writing this book will give you a better version of Mommy. You each possess a distinction that makes you second to none. To my parents, Shadel and Myra Hamilton, you are as solid as they come. Thanks for allowing me to be who I am. Errol McCloud, thank for the gifts of writing, poetry, and our growth together. To all of my siblings and their spouses, you are the best and we excel together.

To you the reader, I want you to experience the freedom that I had while writing this book. I want your greatness to shine brightly, regardless of where you are in your life. While reading, be assured that you can get through and on the other side of anything that presents itself to you. Thank you for digging deeper inside yourself to reveal a greater level of you. There is no one like you!

INTRODUCTION- THE IT

B efore you came to be, God knew your beginning and end. God had a specific purpose in mind when He allowed your mother and father to get together and pro-create. Regardless of your story, regardless of how it happened, planned or not, there is a divine purpose for your existence, and there is absolutely no one like you. Some of you may have heard this before and believe it and some of you may never have accepted it, but I will write it again: "THERE IS NO ONE ELSE LIKE YOU!"

We all are born with a unique DNA and a distinctive stamp on our lives. It is necessary for you to be aware of this distinction and remain authentic, because you possess skills, gifts, and abilities that will change the world in which you live in, the family to which you were born in, and the parents that you were gifted to have. Not all our stories are the same, but it is important to know that no matter what, YOU ARE NECESSARY! YOU ARE VALUABLE! There is no parental manual that will be able to instruct on each child born, as a template is sure to stifle someone's growth and development. There is an assurance that when you arrived on earth, your parents' lives changed and the best instructions for your life will come from the creator. He has orchestrated a well-planned path for your life.

There is an end that has been pre-destined for your life. God set your life in a position to enter the earth realm at a specific time to influence a specific generation and beyond. If you fulfill your purpose, others will know your name for years to come; not because the goal is to be famous, but because you will be popular to those that you have influenced. It is your responsibility to know why you are here and maximize your potential with this knowledge. Be advised; with intention, you will read this more than once on these pages.

The goal of the adversary is to throw you off of that path, to make God out to be a liar.

The goal is also to convince you that you will NEVER measure up to what God spoke about you or to see yourself how He sees you. This is where the struggle between good and evil and the fight of life comes into play.

In my own pursuit and progress of purpose, I've often referred to this passage from Scripture. I remind myself that what I do and who I am is for and in Christ:

> He *"Who hath saved us, and called us with an holy calling, not according to our works, but according to his own purpose and grace, which was given us in Christ Jesus before the world began."* (Timothy 1:9, KJV)

There is no work that offers salvation, but it is a gift that has been freely given by God. I have a personal responsibility to KNOW who I am, ACCEPT who I am, and EXECUTE in faith exactly why I am here.

So, if you have been wondering why you have had some hard times, struggles, and you are still working through them, let me add a little clarity. In part, it is because you are such a threat to the kingdom of darkness, and it is striving to keep you from being unleashed at full potential. So, the pebbles are thrown by the enemy in effort to fight your focus and purpose. Know that you are fully equipped to overcome but we have to throw the little pebbles out of your life.

Undoubtedly, if I took a poll about our lives, we would all view our lives differently, and good or bad can be subjective. This is why I want us to think about purpose, not problems or obstacles. If you see purpose, no matter what comes your way, you will be reminded that there is an aim and goal in your life and there are things that you must complete. You have an expected end designed and suited to fit you. The obstacles that you face can try and change your outlook on life and dismantle your hope. But you and I possess the power and ability to finish what we started and the power to excel.

Everything about you was created wonderfully by God. If you could just imagine with me, for a moment, this straight and smooth path that is designed for you: then comes trouble, insertions, distractions, and voices. Oftentimes, after experiencing those insertions and distractions, we can allow pressure and people's voices to play louder in our hearts and ears than the One that created us. The negative voice and opinion of trouble, the noise of defeat, and the comparative results of those around or before you will become adamant in encouraging the outcome of failure, the outcome of defeat and being a loser. When God created you, He created you strong, with dominion and authority. It is not until you hear a "no" or look at what others around you are doing that you change your posture from confidence to questioning, timidity, and fear: this questioning and second guessing is an entry point, a moment in time and a ploy to get you to forfeit walking in your purpose— with power.

We were made to understand and know God's voice. He has been speaking to us from our inceptions. When we are seeking answers, oftentimes we will go to what is visible; but if we sit and still our minds long enough, there is always the voice of God that yield assurance and does not require a poll from others. That voice will reassure you that *you* will win. The voice of God will speak to you, so we must still and quiet ourselves long enough to hear.

It is in our infancy stage that the enemy wants to throw us off-course so that we don't maximize or reach our God-given purposes.

The enemy of your life and purpose would love for you to focus and stay on the other side of your problems and obstacles, seeing them only as adversities as opposed to crossing over these problems, allowing them to be launching pads for your strength, passion, and momentum. On this path that God has for us, trials and tribulations will come: how we view, process, and handle them will make the difference in what they become and the power they hold in our lives.

If we stay on the hard side of problems, it will be difficult to see ourselves on the side of relief and victory. When we fail to view and process obstacles and adversities the right way, they can become an "IT" in our lives; the start of a cycle of patterns that can, and will, fight our progression, if not ejected by us. Any "IT" that occurs in your life must be fully processed to learn what you should do with the scenario. If not, It can affect the authentic person that God designed of you before there was ever an entry point for trauma, adversity, or offense to enter.

An IT in our lives can be vague or bold. It can be a subtle or a pronounced thing that is presented to throw us off-kilter. We MUST identify what our IT is and go back to its entry point before our IT smashes all of us.

Our lives, our relationships, our communication cannot be defined by an IT— a moment that should pass but instead wants to hang around and define our destinies. We must learn and grow from the interruptions in our lives, not allow them to steal our authenticities, joys, or original designs and characters. The adversities, obstacles, and problems are termed in this book as pebbles in the pond called life. The pond represents a body of water and water, symbolically, represents life.

We will discuss a few common adversities that many of us have, or will face, that wants to affect your life— your pond.

When the pebble has been thrown into the pond (your life), the questions surround what you did with the adversity: Is it hiding in plain sight? Has it merged into the fabric of your being? Did you fully process and resolve conflicts that entered your life? Where is the information? Where is it stored? What part of your life was/ is affected by the pebble?

Growing up in Florida, it was easy to see a body of water; lakes, ponds, beaches, and many puddles. One of the things that I enjoyed as a child was to skip rocks with friends. We would get small pebbles and try to glide them with speed along the top of the water, watching the "waves"—the ripples—emerge. The pebble started in one place, but you would see the ring of waves spread out because of the pebble's interference on that body of water. We, as children, couldn't follow where the last ring disap-peared to nor where the pebble entered; we just saw the ripples spread on the water. We didn't go back and get that pebble out of the pond; we just moved on and found another one to throw again. That is the subtle attempt of the pebble on our purposes: to create such an interference that we cannot find our starting point and allow the pebbles that have already been thrown at us to just sit on the bottom (of our lives) to collect.

Regardless of what has happened in your life, you can rewrite the story. You can overcome; you can see what has occurred and see yourself passing the interruption, past the present moment of that interruption and the pebble thrown at you. To rewrite your story, you must be able to dream and see in faith. See your life as it would be without these problems. I would refer to it as the Miracle life. What would your perfect life look like? This is how you would write your story. You have the power to pen what you can see in faith. You must be able to articulate what you know and see from God, so that you can carry out your purpose. You must possess sight and vision. You must be able to release anything that steals your energy and creativity. There is healthy life on the other side of IT—the pebble in the pond does not have to keep you off-track; you must recognize what IT is, process what has occurred, gain control of your emotions associated with it , and gain momentum to live your best life. Process IT, so that the pebble in your pond cannot gain strength and turn into a boulder in your life's path.

Chapter 1

YOU HAVE PURPOSE

I have spent many years of life in service-related jobs and created a career in human and community services. I've had mentoring groups since I was a teenager. I've started and lead groups in the music community but also served as a stylist and salon manager early in my career. I learned great listening skills at the shampoo bowls. Many shared their vulnerabilities, secrets, adversities and victories. But...my job in health care as an ultra sound tech caused me to be in very close and even more vulnerable places for my patients. As a vascular tech, I've worked in larger hospital settings with the hustle of a fast-paced environment as well as the well-controlled environment of a surgeon's office. But my responsibilities required me to communicate well and was often investigative in nature. I had to build great rapport because I was often asking their life history and had to see many of the patients frequently. I have served in ministry for many years, but I am also a certified life coach and trained victim's advocate. I have been trusted with many stories. Some of what I share in this book is personal, and some is the culmination of experiences after over 25 years of working with people personally. In my evaluation and analysis, I realized that many do not know their purpose, their WHY. They are operating on autopilot through life, not knowing what they should be doing, or they find themselves in a place of discontentment and are still searching to find their way out. This sense of void does not disappear; it will get stronger until you get on the right path...when the greatness in you will yearn to be

1

strengthened and refined by God. The greatness already lies in you; you must be aware of it and be diligent to pursue it.

Merriam-Webster Dictionary defines purpose as "something set up as an object or end to be attained: intention."

Through shared conversations in my career and personal life, I've discovered quite a few people never chose a career that made them happy. They chose what was popular and paid well—and made it work. Ultimately, because it was not something that they deemed purposeful or brought much enjoyment, it has been just that to them—work. Time kept moving at work, but there was a lack of fulfillment to the person.

I've also found that some of these people didn't realize it until later, or until they have invested so much time and energy, that they couldn't see themselves pulling away and starting over with a new career.

Surely, these people made money, met people, and things were still "successful," but there was something missing within themselves. The bills were paid and there was some forward movement in their careers, but there was still yearning from a purpose that cries out and lies in silence while remaining unfulfilled. Is that what denotes success, the fact that one can acquire things? Or, should our success be defined by living out the reason that we were created, walking in obedience to God's will for our lives? It takes all of us to keep the world going around, so we should seek to be in our authentic purposes while doing it-moving in our world. When we move in purpose, our creativity is sharper and more exact. We get more work accomplished because it's innate and you will constantly become the best version of yourself through purpose.

I am not oblivious to the fact that the definition of success varies. Some think if they live in a large home, drive a luxury vehicle, and wear designer clothes, they are successful. Others who have a little apartment, clean laundry, and a bus pass feel they are successful too. I am not here to tell you which of these sides to choose from or to allow this to be your measuring stick of success. I will tell you that you don't have to limit the size of your dreams, but your aspirations must be in alignment with your purpose to experience true success. Success is obedience to that which you are purposed to achieve; that is why you are here on earth. It is an easily embraced fallacy that others' expectations or their standards can define and validate your success to you. What *you* are to be doing for your life and your path defines your success. God called you to a purpose that will not look like anyone else's; you must accept this fact and not aim to be a duplicate of someone else. Although you will have influences in your life and some mentors, you have an authentic DNA that sets you apart and makes you distinct by nature. If you are operating in obedience to what God spoke to you, about your purpose, you have no choice but to experience success, because you are walking in authenticity.

> **You don't have to limit the size of your dreams, but your aspirations must be in alignment with your purpose to experience true success**

"There is a right time for everything, and every-thing on earth will happen at the right time."
(Ecclesiastes 3:1, ERV)

There are many instances where someone did something that became an accepted part of society, creating a standard. Standards and boundaries are necessary, but you have to embrace the fact that you may not fit into the norm of those standards. There are still some that you will carve out and trails that you will blaze; when you do this, you will bless yourself and others. As long as we are alive, ideas, goals, and statuses will vary but you must not become distracted by what others think you should do- you must do what you are purposed to. Our perception becomes our realities, we must declutter and eject things in our lives that can cause our perception to be warped. We must take evaluation and see where our standards derived from because it is necessary to have clarity in our lives, peace in our decisions, and seek out the paths for our authentic purposes.

What I have come to realize is that *things* are not what bring us total satisfaction—it is operating in our purposes that will bring it.

Our responsibility is to know what that something is, the thing that will brand your authenticity and calm your purpose—the meter. It is something that has been with you all along, before you entered your mother's womb and made it to earth. This thing is something that you may be good at with no formal training—you are gifted to do it.

I had a conversation with a woman whose family shared the career trend of journalism and she followed the trend and studied journalism. This career worked well for her family members, but she later realized it was not truly *her* career of choice, although by all appearances she was "successful"—she had connections and experienced great wealth—yet there was something lacking. She desired to be a nurse. The salary was not equal to what she was making, but she took a risk, went back to school, and became a nurse. That's when she came alive. She found her purpose, started doing what she loved, and ended up loving her work. The money was now a bonus and she wasn't a slave to it. She could work as much as she wanted without experiencing the previous level of exhaustion, because she was in the right place, at the right time. She had an impeccable bedside manner and her genuine love for people was evident. She got something that money couldn't buy: the right career choice and working in a place where she was gifted.

When we are out of touch with purpose, it can be exhausting mentally, physically, and emotionally to work, because it requires a greater level of effort. You will put work into your purpose. You will face challenges because you will always be evolving and representing an improved version of yourself, but you will also have the *energy* to do it because it's who you *are inside.*

The only difference between you and your hero, you and those that you see on a platform/stage, is that his/her timing is different. Heroes made it to a platform and grew within themselves. They were confident enough to display their purposes publicly. You possess the same ability to live abundantly in purpose. You must clearly define what purpose is and work it one step at a time to put on display.

Do you have a clear definition of what your purpose is? You cannot allow, "I don't know" to be your answer to this question. This self-discovery of yourself is vitally important to your progression, growth, and development. You will thrive in your purpose and will be a greater asset to those that you are in contact with presently.

If you have that famous answer of "I don't know," then you must ask some basic but very necessary questions of yourself. You will find that you know more than what you give yourself credit for, but you may need to uncover and unclog some channels to your creativity and life. There is a sphere that you must influence with your purpose.

1. What makes you happy?
2. What are you passionate about?
3. Is there some area you would work in even if you never got a paycheck for it and still be fulfilled?
4. What is on your bucket list?
5. If you had a dream job, what would it be?
6. Have you pushed the answers to any of the above questions to the side?
7. How did you choose the career or course of study you are currently in?
8. Do you have a passion for a certain group of people? (I.e. children, teens, geriatrics, men, women.)

If you can't get past question one, please don't be discouraged: you may have to keep pushing forward.

Chapter 2

IN TIME

W e all possess hidden and manifested talents. There are strengths, gifts, and abilities we are not aware of that rise at certain times in our lives, when we need them or simply in their proper timing, and we are able to handle them.

> *I will praise thee; for I am fearfully and wonder-*
> *fully made: marvelous are they works; and that*
> *my soul knoweth right well. My substance was*
> *not hid from thee, when I was made in secret, and*
> *curiously wrought in the lowest parts of the earth.*
> *Thine eyes did see my substance, yet being unper-*
> *fect; and in thy book all my members were written,*
> *which in continuance were fashioned, when as yet*
> *there was none of them."* (Psalms 139 14 -16, KJV)

God is not trying to figure out what to do with you—He did that already. God is not confused about who you are; He knows what your life should look like. Sometimes the conflict comes from embracing what your life is to *Him*, as opposed to what *you* think it should look like. Your influences and what you were exposed to, your geographical location and the era that you were born in, all frame your thoughts of what your life should look like.

There is always a popular thing in a specific time; the fad, the thing that many are doing. The pressure of society shows you the highest-paying jobs, the most popular fields, and the opinions of others, as opposed to that assurance in your heart. What about the thing that you spent years as a child investing in and then you "outgrew" it, or the "nice but won't pay the bills" thing, or the "I love it, but it's not popular" thing? What about making *those* things work where you are? That thing has always been present.

How much are you willing to go back and explore of your interests? When you dust off the things that you tucked away in yourself, you will find some of the hidden treasures.

If we allow the opinions of people to drown out the voice of God, we are already off-track. There are some things that you think about, dream about, sketch out, and want to see happen, but you won't share it with others for fear of someone knocking the idea down. You may be that person in your family that chooses a career no one in your circle has embarked upon before. It makes you feel like an outcast; it may make you get talked about—but is it the good and acceptable will of God for your life?

> *But as it is written, Eye hath not seen, nor ear heard, neither have entered into*
> *the heart of man, the things which God hath pre-pared for them that love him.*
>
> *But God hath revealed them unto us by his Spirit: for the Spirit searcheth all things, yea, the deep things of God."* (1 Corinthians 2:9-10, KJV)

Some things in your life require you to alleviate the opinions of others. Some decisions you cannot share because they are not popular with others. Nevertheless, there is a passion crying out, a purpose yearning for fulfillment in you. In the Bible, at the time Noah began talking about rain, it had not happened before. God knew that it would come and that He would use Noah as an answer for the people, but all in its proper time. Noah had a word from the Lord and a sure plan to go with that word. Even if what you must do makes you look crazy to people, it's safer to go the God route. We would rather be obedient to the voice of God, because He is not going to leave us hanging and He knows our end from the beginning.

Joseph had a dream and shared it with others, and it brought on some envy, jealousy, and personal attacks from others. His position as the youngest son in his family caused people to hate him, as did the devotion that his father displayed for him. Joseph had no control over his place in his family, but as he began to identify things about himself, he shared them. Unfortunately, it was with those that did not have the capacity to see, hold, or promote it, so they fought it—they fought him. Please don't expect all to support what you see; after all, it's your vision, and dream, and your capacity is different from others. Living in purpose may not always make you feel comfortable, but you will be fulfilled and in alignment with God.

When your decisions and verbiage are not common amongst or popular with those around you, you may experience some resistance. Some of this resistance is not personal; it's just unfamiliar to the crowd. However, we must all remember that we are called to live the uncommon life. We are made from an individual design that complements each other appropriately, not cut from a template. Joseph's family did not like that he was bold enough to speak his dream, and they undoubtedly did not understand what he was speaking because it was not yet time for the dream to manifest. (Genesis 37:5-8) If God has called you to do something, He will give specific instructions and will always have those assigned to support, assist, and help to launch the vision with you. It just may not be who you think it is. Your help may not come from your local or familiar resources. Walking in purpose will cause you to change, transform, and constantly evolve. If you have people in your circle that have categorized your success and limited your abilities, it will always cause agitation when they cannot make you a puppet. You must be willing to cut the strings to ensure you are on the right stage. Joseph's brothers sold him into slavery, but they could not have fully understood what they were doing. They heard what Joseph was saying, but they only saw him in his present state.

Although your purpose is always present, you have to be at a place of maturity in time to handle it and execute it well. Moving in something prematurely can prove to be disastrous and create a level of stress that is not necessary for you. Similar to a relationship with our children. When our children see us executing things in our lives, they think that they can do it the same.

Our teenager is starting to drive, and, in our practicing, I've explained that driving is a serious matter. I have made him aware of all of the things he must pay attention to, including the silent communications called signs. I illuminated the importance of being able to read and understand street signs, watching for sirens and lights, and paying close attention to the other drivers. He quickly realized that what we made look easy requires more skill than what it seemed. Although he has been riding in a car all of his life, he saw us put the keys in and operate the vehicle, getting to and from various points. If he had attempted to drive the car sooner than now, it could have proven to be disastrous. He may not have been able to see over the steering wheel or focus on all of the moving parts. But he studied the book portion of driving, and we are merely helping him to accomplish and refine something that he has been seeing all of his life. Your purpose has been with you all of your life and you may have been operating in some facets of it, but there is a time where you will blossom and grow leaps and bounds because it is the proper time. Walking in purpose will secure a future for you and those to whom you serve. Your walking in authentic purpose can change your world and your family and friends. Although Joseph's family could not identify it at the time, he was the one to help secure their future. With all the resistance, lies, and hardships, he knew God was using him for the greater good, to save many. Once you identify your purpose, you must be willing to embrace the process, work out the details, and follow it to completion. Joseph was sure of his dream; he did not allow the lack of acceptance to make him put it away. He was willing to stand on the vision and move forward. He did not have the details of the adversity that would present after sharing his dream. He didn't know in advance that he would get such a reaction from his family. I could only imagine that the brothers thought that their abuse would kill the dreamer in Joseph- silence him, but it didn't. Joseph experienced great trauma from his family, he was in uncomfortable situations, but those incidents-interruptions did not kill his gift. The trauma and interruptions could not eradicate his purpose. In time, he realized the dream, and vision were larger than he could ever imagine.

There are areas in your life that are not always visible until certain times. There are gifts that can lie dormant in certain environments, only to awaken and thrive in others. When there is a need for an answer to the problem, your purpose meter alerts you. You must know what these things are, and stay open to the discovery of greater endeavors, because you will increase in purpose. When you know who you are, others cannot tell you who you are not. When you know what you are to do, you must run after it. You do not need anyone to validate you—that happened in the beginning with God, and your first breath verified it.

When you know who you are, others cannot tell you who you are not

1. What are your strengths and gift areas?
2. What have you been dreaming about, visualizing?
3. What areas do you want to strengthen?
4. What are some things that currently frustrate you? Can you create a solution?
5. Do you feel limited in a particular area? Please explain.
6. Have you shrunk or diminished based on something you heard or experienced?

7. Have you ever been rejected? Explain where and how it made you feel. What can you learn from this?
8. Are you an exhorter of potential?
9. Do you like to host events?
10. Are you gifted in administration and logistics skills?
11. What would your life look like without an obstacle?
12. If money wasn't an object, what would you do for a career?
13. Where would you attend school?
14. Would you go to college?
15. What city would you live in?
16. Have you accomplished any part of the goals that you dream about?

These questions are to enable you to assess some areas and expound beyond the pressure from society.

Chapter 3

PURPOSE MUST BE IDENTIFIED EARLY

E arlier we asked the questions, What is your purpose? What makes you happy? What were you created to do? Some of us can't answer what makes us happy; we can't articulate what we like to do. If we are not careful, we can find ourselves moving, busy but lacking production. It doesn't mean that you aren't doing good things, but are you maximizing your potential? Are you expanding, or are you a cycle of the same thing? What are you creating? What new challenges have you accepted? What have you overcome? What have you done in the last 90 days that has changed your life, or someone else's, for the better?

The reality of your responsibilities can cause you to be busy: mother, father, family backbone, corporate executive, breadwinner at the home, educator, wife, husband, leader, student, support staff. All of these are very important and necessary positions, but none of these should make you lose your identity as an individual that you had before you gained these responsibilities and roles. Before any responsibility, there was you. You came out and someone was there to nurture you. You were able to rest and have basic needs met in balance. If this was your beginning, then it should remain an important part of your life going forward. In order to keep a balanced you, there has to be an identified you. You must know what makes you smile, what's important, and how to keep these truths in balance. You must know what is necessary and a priority for your life and the space that you are in. You must know the resolution that you are to offer someone or something. What are you the answer to?

Purpose aligns with your roles, as God knows all aspects of your life. He knew what He would bless you with, but that does not mean He wants you to neglect your purpose, your gifts, or your talents. You are to be able to do all of it well. The way that you will accomplish tasks is to have a clearly defined purpose in front of you.

WHAT are your priorities in life? Name at least five.

_____

_____

_____

_____

_____

Now look up to see where you are on the list. Are you *on* the list?

We are not talking about denying your responsibilities but making a conscious effort to realize your lifeboat can't deflate as you try to rescue everyone else. To be your best for anyone, self-care is important.

**Whatever your role, your purpose
should enhance it!**

If you are gifted as a leader or teacher, it should affect how you operate in your other, various roles. The teacher will have a special approach as a parent or will rise in the ranks of a company, but you must know that you are a teacher in whatever role. Undoubtedly, it could have always been a part of your personality. Your family may have noticed it in your toddler years, but it may not have been viewed as what it would become. Children are often silenced when their natural gifts and abilities are dominant in their early years because their gifts can be easily misunderstood. This is not always the case, but I have seen it enough times, which is why I will insert here that it is important for us to ask God how to parent, mentor, and nurture those that are in our spheres of influence. If we only perform our roles based on a cultural template, we can shut down the emerging genius in someone and insert an unnecessary fight. These fights can be ejected by stopping cycles of limitations, learning to recognize gifts and abilities early, not restricting them solely based on age and tradition. We have to learn how to identify purpose personally and as a community.

Our daughter loves to work in the kitchen. She loves to bake and cook. Although she can barely see over the stove, I still include her in the activities that are safe for her and allow her to assist with my guidance. I am a teacher, so it's my responsibility to teach at her level and not simply shut her down because of her age. All is not a YES, but all is not a NO. We adjust to allow the lessons to be learned and hone a consistent interest that incorporates the natural artist that she is. I also purchase things that she can do on her own to strengthen her confidence in this area. I am present to instruct her, but allow her to operate in safety with some independence.

The full blossom of this gift may not be ready now, but she still has to nurture it along the way.

While writing this book, I came into contact with an individual that confirmed the very thought of this chapter. We began to discuss our passions and lives, and I asked her, "How did you know that you wanted to be a physician?" She told me that she was always in love with science. However, culturally, there was a push to be a physician or an engineer; those are two of the acceptable careers in her culture, but science was a natural thing for her. She cultivated her love for science and initially planned to be a pediatrician, but later realized this would not be good for her. She was fortunate to have those in her family that were physicians and she could eliminate the specialty that she wanted to pursue along the way. She also noted that she had a great and influential mentor in the specialty field she ultimately decided to pursue. Her mentor gave her information that she knew was over her head, but she knew that the gift and passion was there in the lady; her purpose was identified. In our conversation, she confirmed that she loves her job. The other medical specialties may have afforded her some other perks, but she is happy where she is. Another family member of hers, on the other hand, was encouraged to pursue the same careers, engineering or medicine/science as culture states, but this was not a natural path for her. Although the family member is good at many things, she has not settled on the thing that drives her and is still searching. I'm sure that she will find her path, but it may not look like what everyone else suggests, as purpose must be identified.

It's important to know who you are inside so that you don't work in the wrong place. In everything that you do, purpose should be in focus. You may have to shift and change some things around to juggle the hats you wear, but you should still know what makes you happy so that when you get a break from various responsibilities, you know what to do; or while you are in these roles, you don't lose focus on your WHY. If you don't do what makes you happy, or suppress it, it's easy to take on an inauthentic personality; you learn to become *what* you do, as opposed to becoming and sharpening who you are. You can start to move on autopilot and can lose sight of the expected end.

> **"For I know the thoughts that I think toward you, saith the Lord, thoughts of peace, and not of evil, to give you and expected end."** (Jeremiah 29:11, KJV)

I choose the role of parent to expound upon because it's an area of great juggling in many of our lives. "I have to walk in and fulfill my purpose, but I have others that are totally dependent on me." This is one of the greatest reasons why you can't back down on what you are assigned to do as a parent. The purpose that you pursue will bless you and your children. Your obedience to walk in purpose affects your inheritance. We are blessed to lead the lives of children and how we do it sets in motion the future of our world. What a great and heavy responsibility, but this role alone should encourage you to know how powerful you are. If you are a parent, then you realize the sacrifice of everything. We don't get to quit parenting and regardless of what is on our plate, we must parent, we must train and teach, because we are born to do it. No one must teach an animal how to parent, as it's an innate ability; the same with mankind.

Your obedience to walk in purpose affects your inheritance

What can you articulate to your children about your life, your roles? How can you help them to set goals and standards by what goals you present? Parenting is one of the roles in life in which we are most influential; children won't mimic what you say but what they see you do. We must give our children guidelines to follow. Even if you are not a parent, your presence still influences children. You have the option to shape and sharpen or suppress and stifle. The reality is that you are influencing someone, for good or bad. I think of the children in our society where cycles of dysfunction and purpose crises can be perpetuated until we make a conscious effort to identify them. Purpose must be identified clearly and concisely. If you present a clear and concise path, it is easier to give the generation watching you something worthwhile to see.

Purpose must be identified clearly and concisely

We should all evolve from our point of origination, but there should be a sure foundation first for what you are growing into and becoming. It is easier to nurture our younger generation from the beginning, as opposed to trying to overthrow things that have grown within us and oppose our true identities. When we, as adults, know our strengths, weaknesses, and identified purposes, we are able to parent/teach with more excellence. And we will know what to refrain from that does not fit into that. We don't have to leave our learning to trial and error if we put structure and strategy in place.

If you consider areas where you are gifted or where you are passionate, you would choose jobs or hobbies differently. Life isn't meant for us to wander aimlessly through it; we are to be intentional and execute our lives well. Our purpose is to be fortified and secured in the things God created us to do. He made everything well, so our ideas and visions should line up with His. To prosper is what we are created to do, and we do that in purpose. Our blossoming and growth are the intentions.

Some things can be identified by noticing interests in people. Many children love to play with dolls, but some are drawn to different things about that doll. One may like to change its clothes, or its hair, or enjoy talking to it. There is something about the purpose in the individual that will cry out in that scenario. If it's the clothes, do you see this interest in any other place? How do you hone this? Do you put the child in arts and crafts? Do you take the child to fashion shows? We may not know in totality what this interest will yield, but it shouldn't be ignored. We want to nurture healthy behaviors. Purpose will always cry out of us because it is why we are here.

> *"Train up a child in the way he should go; and when he is old, he will not depart from it."*
> *(Proverbs 22:6 KJV)*

What blueprints are we creating for purpose to be identified in our infancy stages? We have to know our purpose so that we can help teach about purpose to future generations.

> *"And he shall be like a tree planted by the rivers of water, that bringeth forth his fruit in his season; his leaf also shall not wither; and whatsoever he doeth shall prosper."* *(Psalms 1:3 KJV)*

WHO you are and what you do affects so much more than just you. When you are in your purpose, you can affect those that you are assigned to. I intentionally repeat this because operating in your purpose irresponsibly is something we cannot do.

Let's think about a tree for a moment. A tree has a lot character: it's strong, supportive, giving, beautiful, and productive. A tree is deeply rooted to stand against various weather patterns. It endures sunshine, winds, storms, and pruning, but it is not confused that it is a tree. Its posture denotes that it is a tree; its parts suggest the same. Every part of the tree is vitally important to its existence and production.

The tree adds beauty, adds oxygen, bears fruit, and provides shade. It supports human life as well as animal life. Some animals take shelter in trees and find them to be places of safety. The tree is not looking at the other trees, because it's too busy producing. There are times when the tree is resting. Leaves must fall off so that new ones can come. It must change colors to denote the seasons. We depend on trees for more than we give them credit. For some, the wood from the trees provide heat and the ability to cook. There are so many different responsibilities and trees can perform all of them because it was made to be a tree; it's in its identity and DNA to be a tree.

Not all trees look alike; they are different in geographical locations. Palm trees can't survive the harshness of winter and the bitter cold, but a good ole oak can stand tall. All of the trees begin with a seed; a seed that must be cared for and nurtured along the way. How it starts does not exemplify all that it will become. It is important to know WHOM we are and what we are called to do, with assurance. When you know this truth first, then you will be able to meet all your responsibilities with excellence. Even when changes arise and adjustments are necessary, you must hold to the assurance of who you are. You are a tree that must bring forth fruit and in your proper season.

Once purpose is identified, it requires constant progression. Just as the trees provide oxygen, your place in purpose will be fresh air, being a breath of life to others. When you stand tall as the tree, you help to produce life for generations. You will inspire others and create personal happiness and fulfillment for them. Your work and impartation start as a seed in the life of others that have the capacity to grow into a beautiful tree that will provide for generations to come. Your productivity will help you to operate in personal happiness and fulfillment. This world requires all of us to operate in authenticity to keep a good, healthy balance of life.

1. Who are you?
2. What are your current roles?
3. What kind of people do you attract?
4. How can you tell someone else to care for you?
5. How can you promote a healthy balance on this earth and in your personal world?
6. If you were to assess the people in your life can you identify gifts that can be nurtured that will help bring clarity of their existence?
7. Can you look at the young people in your life and see some of their strengths?

Chapter 4

WHAT DO YOU POSSESS?

I t is extremely important to know what you possess so that you will not sell yourself short. When you can identify your good, know your value and worth, and convey it to others, then you are aware and can live in personal integrity that will foster healthy relationships.

> When you can identify your good, know your value and worth, and convey it to others, then you are aware and can live in personal integrity that will foster healthy relationships

At what do you excel? What can you do effortlessly? What can you do without formal training? What were you born to do?

I was sharing a conversation with one of my sister-friends about her daughter, a beautiful and successful model who started modeling as a baby. I said to her mother, "This is who she is." This is what she was meant to do, you could detect the capacity for this in her behavior early. I can recall our conversations about her robust and brave personality as an infant. I witnessed her walk around with beads on her neck and a sharp fashion sense as a toddler. She has always possessed character and finesse. Thankfully, her parents were able to identify these gifts and began to nurture them. They had her involved in what was natural for her and today, she has a successful career as a model, constantly sought after by companies. Kudos to her parents for recognizing what she possessed and for honing the skills.

In Scripture, Esau, the eldest son of Isaac and Rebekah, sold his birthright to his younger brother Jacob for a pot of stew. (Genesis 25:31) The significance of birthright was devalued. One must question if Esau really knew what he possessed, especially to give it up so easily. He was tired from being in the field, and Jacob knew that. Esau acted out of impulse, which would affect his life, his goods, his inheritance, and his position. Being mentally and spiritually weighed down doesn't mean you should allow the enemy to catch you off-guard and respond to things abruptly, without discernment. Some of what you fight, in your mind or environment, has a goal to weigh you down so that you are distracted from your original design and purpose.

You cannot allow yourself or others to diminish your value. When we are sure of what we possess of skills and talents, our entire world and perspective changes.

> *"Thus saith the Lord, thy Redeemer, the Holy One of Israel; I am the Lord thy God which teacheth thee to profit, which leadeth thee by the way that thou shouldest go."* (Isaiah 48:17, KJV)

What you possess is more valuable than your current emotional state. What you possess will affect generations to come, so it's your responsibility to nurture and maximize what you possess. There is so much good in you, so you must know what it is and effectively communicate it to others. What you possess gives you the power to grow in your relationships and helps others to do the same. Esau could not have thought about the long-term effects of his impulsive decision. What he possessed was not worth just giving it away. He was in the presence of someone that knew what he possessed but wanted it for himself. Esau's desperation allowed him to entertain someone that had no good intentions towards him. You must share and invest your time, gifts, talents, and treasures with those that value YOU. There will always be those present that want to undermine you and want you to shrink from your goals, but you can't afford that. The danger in shrinking your gifts is that you don't know what you will lose in the process, including your peace. The manipulative person will always expect you to shrink, with a hope to lord over you, and then you enter an unhealthy relationship with him/her. In that moment where Jacob propositioned Esau about the pot of stew in exchange for his birth-right Esau chose to shrink to satisfy an immediate need. His need for food didn't allow him to see the value of his birthright in full detail. He had been in the field all day and wanted an answer to his issue. Jacob had an answer but it was not the right one for Esau. In this instance Jacob was a manipulator of Esau's vulnerability. This was by no means an even exchange but Jacob knew the value and Esau didn't honor it-what he possessed.

Sometimes when you are experiencing the feeling of being weighed down, it's easy to want to respond abruptly to situations, but this is the perfect time to think through things carefully and not make important decisions. What if Esau had put more thought into what was proposed by Jacob? Could the outcome have been different for him? When you are mentally exhausted it can be tempting to isolate yourself; but this is the time when you must surround yourself with those that know your value and worth. Surround yourself with those that have the capacity to hold you up and speak life and strength to you and refrain from those that will take advantage of your vulnerabilities. There will be times in your life when you need alone time, but you must know when to come back, connect, and plug in with others. Through this, you guard yourself from SNEAK ATTACKS.

Sneak attacks are the mind weights, negative words, and failures that love to surface in your mind when you are down. Therefore, we must clean off the hard drive of our minds and emotions so that any residual pain and weighted memories will not emerge and have power over us in a weakened state. When you are account-able and honest about where you are, how you feel, and what you need, you remove any power from the sneak attack. Sneak attacks can cause you to make abrupt decisions that you could find your-self regretting later.

I want you to think for a moment about your life and in moments of difficulty and adversity it can feel like you are in the wilderness. This is probably not your most desirable state. But just like in the wilderness, animals are safer in a pack. If there is danger of a threat or impending attack, the offender will have to go through more than one animal. It is the same in your life- if someone throws a pebble in the pack, there are multiple eyes and ears at work and, therefore, a greater line of defense. Jacob threw a pebble and Esau had to deal with the ripple effects that it would cause in his life. But in this instance, Esau made a choice. Was he too tired from being in the field? How successful was his day of hunting? Did Jacob catch him in a depressed state? We could only imagine the answers to these questions but what we do know is that Esau did not see the value of his birthright, so he sold it. Esau experi-enced a sneak attack! Jacob approached him away from a support system and at a time of vulnerability. Knowing what you possess will help you prioritize what you need and when. Knowing what you possess will cause you to work on your skills. Knowing what you possess with sharpen your discernment and help you to gage when to say yes or no. Esau could have waited a little longer for food and he had the capacity to hunt for it. He was a skilled hunter. You must be cautious not to allow a temporary moment or situ-ation to cause you to forfeit your purpose and greatness. This is why it is imperative to define what you possess.

If you know what you possess you will still face challenges but the possession will not change.

You may be tempted to "dumb down" what you possess, due to the fear of failure or lack of acceptance—but you don't need to do so. You don't have a reason to retreat from your purpose assignment;

after all, it is why you are here. When you experience rejection and uncertainty in your life, it can cause you to have a fear of failure. When you are unsure about what you should be doing and how to do it, you can encounter a fear of failure. Truthfully, no one wants to be unsuccessful, and you don't know all the pieces in your journey, but you *must* leap and try.

Comparing our lives to others and making someone else's standards our own heightens our feelings of failure about ourselves. If you are still moving and trying tasks, then you have not failed. You may need to take an assessment of yourself, but still know you are making progress: just don't stop trying. Embrace your distinct nature and you will quickly see how successful you can become.

Although it happens at different points in our lives, I think it's normal to want to be accepted: accepted on the basketball, swim, or football teams; accepted among your peers; acknowledged and rewarded for your efforts. However, you don't want to seek acceptance to the point where you look for validation from people and the things that you do all the time. Your acceptance must come from who you are and what you possess from God's perspective. You can't stop doing what God tells you to because someone else can't see it in you. If your acceptance of self is based on man's validation, then you can be controlled and yo-yoed like a puppet forever. Be willing to own what you possess so that you are not quick to give it away to others. Esau dealt with the pressures and consequences of giving away his birthright to his brother. Yes, he still saw blessings and success in his life, but it came with a greater level of hardship than what God had originally intended.

1. What has been weighing you down?
2. What has been your greatest victory in your life?
3. Do you feel like something was taken from you?
4. What are the parts of you that you chose to dumb down to make someone feel comfortable or to be accepted?
5. If given 30 seconds tell me three wonderful things about you.

Chapter 5

THE IT OF TRAUMA

In earlier chapters, I began to talk about the IT of life. It's simple...I want to challenge you to Identify IT, be able to define IT, confront IT, and overcome IT, so that you live as authentically as possible—and it *is* possible. Your IT will be anything that took you off course from your purpose; the reason you exist. Whether it be trauma, rejection suppression, negative words, brokenness, violation, or anything of the like, to be able to operate in true purpose and authenticity, you need to realize and recognize IT. If you don't realize the need for improvement or change in yourself, it will be difficult for you to do so. Whatever you've been exposed to, good or bad, defines your norms. Some of the words mentioned above may have been commonly experienced in your environment and haven't been challenged by you. This allows adverse behavior to sneak into the corners of your life and potentially strengthen with every incident that resembles what you initially experienced. Even in a situation where you have seen negative or adverse things repeated, there is truth on the inside of you that will let you know that something is off or in conflict. If you ignore making changes, you can shape and build your life on what you have accepted, as opposed to what is genuine and your authentic purpose.

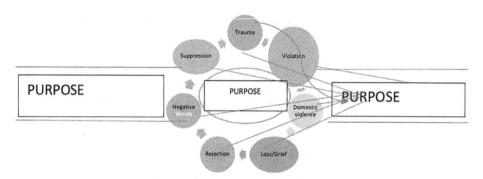

PURPOSE

PURPOSE

PURPOSE

(Figure 1.) Life originating on the path of purpose and then interruptions come. The goal is to get to the other side of the obstacle and back on track with purpose. Purpose can be smaller within this cycle if the entry points are not addressed.

God has a path for you but when trouble comes, it creates a point of entry or offense to appear; it takes you off course of your purpose. You will experience an identity crisis if this entry point is embraced as normal and is nurtured. Then, the trauma of a negative incident would begin to frame your identity, as opposed to God's original design for you framing your identity.

Sometimes the trauma can make you count yourself out in situations, causing you to have self-diminishing thoughts or take on an inauthentic identity of yourself. The trouble can cause you to become guarded and create a safety net so that you refrain from pain. Trauma can happen at such an early start in your life that it can become all you know of yourself. When an offense sits so long in your mind without resolution, it can be difficult to recognize the acute issues that arose from it.

The Substance Abuse and Mental Health Services Administration (SAMHSA) describes individual trauma as resulting from:

> an **event**, series of events, or set of circumstances that is **experienced** by an individual as physically or emotionally harmful or life threatening and that has lasting adverse **effects** on the individual's functioning and mental, physical, social, emotional, or spiritual well-being.

If you have experienced trauma, it's a life-altering event and is the reason you must stop and start over. Gather yourself together— the "you" prior to the event —and resume your life. When trauma happens, we must deal with it and heal so that we don't create a cycle. For example, if you grew up in an abusive family, you may accept abuse as normal until you see a healthier alternative to it. Conditioning one's mind may have occurred to make incest normal to the person, for instance if it occurred in their family. When we accept trauma as normal, it becomes easy to perpetuate the behaviors in our homes and communities. Any cycle of trauma will continue until it is stopped.

The worst trauma that anyone of us can experience is our own. It does not matter if others think it's the worst or not—your trauma is your truth. What you feel about your pain is your reality.

Your body, emotions, and insight know when things are off, something that was traumatic for one may not resonate as such with another. Any trauma that happens in your life can throw you off course. There are physiological, as well as psychological, things that happen when a person experiences trauma, which are some of the main reasons we cannot smother and ignore everything that happens to us.

What we have been exposed to can help to create a tolerance or level of acceptance in us, until we experience something different, such as growth and development, that changes what we experienced.

When you can identify your good, know your value and worth, and convey it to others, then you are aware and can live in personal integrity that will foster healthy relationships

I remember taking a class in advocacy and we were discussing domestic violence. While teaching, one of the counselors gave information on how domestic violence can be viewed across various races. She stated that oftentimes the battered victims made excuses for the offender, or they felt like they should take the abuse to show strength. I believe that this does not allow for victims to come to a resolve of trauma in this area.

Community expectations and some historical and generational behaviors induce this level of tolerance. Sometimes only after we're out of a scenario do we see what's off about it, in which the damage is already done. I'm hoping we can create healthy dialogues and utilize available resources to recognize and repair the damage in someone. Illuminating the fact, that although trauma may be present, there is life on the other side of the matter.

Many external factors shape our thought patterns about our lives and what they should look like. I'm hoping that we can declutter enough of those patterns so that internal voice of God will be louder than any external influence. This is the voice that trials, tribulations, mistakes, and less-than-perfect scenarios want to drown out. Since most of us don't know what that uninterrupted, perfect scenario looks like, we must roll with the punches and play the hand that we are dealt. In life, we all face some type of conflict or adversity, but how we withstand and overcome those situations is the skill that we want to develop and continually sharpen in life.

Trauma can happen at any age. The things that happen in our parents' lives have an effect on us from the time we are in the womb, forming and growing. Some people experience uneventful pregnancies and then there are those that are high risk for various reasons. Some parents are excited about the new bundle that is soon to come, while others instantly or later reject parenthood. Whether we want to acknowledge it or not, the human that is growing inside of a woman is able to feel the effects of the parent's environment. Oftentimes we see a response, a kick, a twirl, and sometimes an entire shift in the woman's extended belly as the child is spoken to in the womb. Especially in the latter part of the pregnancy, we can see more reaction from the baby in utero with the naked eye and even more with ultrasound technology.

I was about five months pregnant with our daughter while I was having an ultrasound. This time, they were doing a 3-D ultrasound and the technician and I were talking. I began to laugh at something said and she captured my daughter doing the same. I shared this image with my husband and with a few family members. Our daughter Ju Ju (as we affectionately call her) still displays the same behavior with me. There are times where my laughter gets her attention like no one else's and she often chuckles with me. My husband notes, "She has been doing this since being in the womb." Similarly, we knew she would love to dance because of the display of behavior … in the womb. There were many things that we saw before she was ever physically in our arms that match the personality that she has now… and it is BIG. We ask God for wisdom to lead and guide her for the purpose that He has created for her. We have some insight on some of her gifts, but I am certain we have not seen all of them yet. It is a part of parental responsibility to nurture and protect her, to guard her from unnecessary trauma and pain. Because God gifted her to us, we are to help those in her village (community) to know how to nurture her as well, as we must do for all of our children and those that are in our care. It's important to build strong foundations in our youth so that if they are faced with adversity, there is a confidence present to fortify their core. Trauma can shake one at the core.

Some of the ITs in our lives started in the womb and we must go back that far. Some have said, "I've been like this all my life." Well, that is because you came out fighting and you did not throw the first blow. The good news is that God does not go back on His Word: however, there are some external factors that rooted early and grew in your life, ultimately affecting your purpose, destiny, and peace.

31

We must uproot all things that are contrary to what God has created you for and what He has spoken about your existence. This is one reason we must heal and think about the things that we say and do with our youth, because they grow up with those things, whether good or bad. Sometimes we welcome an unnecessary fight by allowing entry points of trauma/uncertainty at infancy. If it's important to protect your eye and ear gates as an adult, it's much more important to do so for our children, even in utero. We can't act like our children aren't in the room or the womb, just because they can't participate at a certain level. We must create safeguards against trauma at their inception. So, any points of trauma from pregnancy and beyond must be ejected right away so that children can blossom, flourish, and prosper. Some of the unknown things that you have been fighting, that you can't trace, could have made their entrances when you were in the womb.

All of us were made in God's image. All of us have been given dominion, power, and the ability to prosper and do well. We can't allow trauma and risky events to totally define lives because we possess the ability to overcome and live beyond the trauma.

> *"So they grow strong, like a tree planted by a stream—a tree that produces fruit when It should and has leaves that never fall. Everything they do is successful."* (Psalm 1:3, ERV)

I was about ten years old when my family experienced a traumatic event, the loss of my uncle who was brutally murdered. His death was hard enough to deal with, but because of the nature of the crime and the complexity of the case, all of the families in the community were directly affected and immediately homeless.

Aunts, uncles, cousins, and my immediate family were in a whirlwind, needed a new place to live, and having to deal with the emotions of tragically losing a loved one. We immediately had to uproot our lives, change schools, and relocate to Grandma's house as we waited on help from the Red Cross. We needed support to find new housing. All this affected us greatly, since our uncles were our male role models and because several of us were in single-mother homes. I remember hearing the concerned chatter about the effect our loss would have on the boys in my family, because our uncle took so much time with them, but we all had to receive some type of therapy to process this level of pain.

The trauma literally shifted everything. All that was normal for us became nonexistent. Many of the families that had grown up together and built a healthy community were now separated.

I remember going to a new school and having to start over. One of the things that I recall was the challenge of adjusting to a new school.

I left a school with good friends and a great social environment to come to one where I did not easily fit in. At the time, I only wore dresses to school and that made me stick out like a sore thumb. Within the first few days, one of the pretty, popular girls walked up to me and said, "I just want you to know that I don't like you." I replied firmly, "I don't care." Nonetheless, can you imagine the pressure involved, being new and disliked by one of the favorites in school?

To create a distaste for girls, my own kind, was a trick that the enemy wanted to work; a seed that he hoped would take root and, for a little while, it worked.

I later realized that the enemy of my destiny was aiming at further down the line of my life, with my ability to be effective with women. Over the years I have mentored and coached many women. I have formed and led several support groups and organizations for women. If this previous moment as a child had not been challenged I may have not been able to form these groups. I was too young to fully understand what this attempt on my future could have done, but I came to understand it better-later.

This pebble was thrown at me from girls (women) and I found myself gravitating more to guys because I was comfortable with them. This was so because I had to co-exist with them in my family environment anyway. I am the first-born granddaughter with three boys prior and a few right behind me, so boys were normal. They made me tough and they protected me.

Although I was comfortable with the male species, with no ulterior motive, I realized that others did not view things the same way I did. I had to learn how to interact with men in a different manner, and over the years tried to teach it to others. The very thing that I was using to protect myself still came with pressure, and the very thing I was using to protect myself could have boomeranged back against me.

The goal of the adversary is the same: to kill, steal, and destroy. (John 10:10) If he could have gotten me to forfeit the ministry for women from that seed of offense or entry point made earlier in my life, he would have been satisfied. I eventually got just as involved at that new school as I was at the other. Now, to some this may seem like child's play, but you must consider seeds we have and the kinds of trees they can produce. I was fortunate enough to have a good support system at home that helped me to pro-cess some of the adverse moments, and it better prepared me for when I dealt with similar behaviors as a teenager and adult. One entry point can cause a ripple effect of trauma in a person. This point was trying to affect ministry, create self-hatred, hatred of my own kind, and the inability to form healthy relationships. We cannot hate who we are. I am a woman—I cannot walk around hating women, or deal with them harshly because of trauma or an improperly healed wound. I have used my testimony in several of my workshops in rooms full of women, as I know God had to heal this area for me, because I experienced several, similar, traumatic scenarios throughout life. I am sure I am not the only one.

I am blessed to say that I have long-term, healthy relationships with women, some whom I have been friends with since grade school. There are still circles that I will never fit into and I am okay with that. I wish I could say that as an adult, I've never experienced the same behavior as when I was ten years old from women - but that's not true. I can recognize others as wounded and guarded just as I was because of trauma in their lives. This form of social trauma can spill over into other areas of life. Sometimes we make these relationship dynamics a normal part of life when they shouldn't be. It is behavior that must be ejected, so we won't continue cycles.

The loss of our uncle was tragic, and it had a huge effect on his children and all our family members. A certain level of anger surrounded the scenario: there was community distrust, there were some who wanted revenge, and many who were left desolate. The way that trauma can perpetuate negative behavior is to be stuck in that moment and hold all the resentment, anger, and distrust inside.

My grandmother played a major role in our healing. Although she lost her son and said often "There is no pain like losing a child," she advocated for peace. She created a safe space for her family to live, to talk about what was happening; she prayed us through the tragedy, and one of her biggest moves was the lack of hatred and great amount of compassion she showed for the one that murdered her child. She told the attorney, "I am not asking for the death penalty. I am not the giver of life and I don't want to have control of taking someone's life. He is someone's son." Although her son was gone, she did not want another mother to experience her pain. She took her pain and processed it and coached us in healing as well. Grandma's display of love is what we all must obtain; she didn't want anyone to be wounded by our trauma. Like Grandma, choosing this decision will help us to become free and healed.

From a physiological standpoint, trauma and crisis are noted for throwing your brain offline until you deactivate its hold on you. Sure, the circumstances may not go away, but you can strip the control and power of it from your ability to move forward. If you are offline ... you have the capacity and potential to get back in, get unstuck, and operate at full capacity. Once you are aware that a traumatic event has occurred in your life, you must now ask the question, Where is it? What did you do with the information, the moment, the event; where is it stored? What part of your life was/ is affected by a traumatic event? You do not have to normalize anything that made you feel violated or caused an interruption in your life, but it is important to do a brain dump and rid yourself of this event that will try to hide in your life and control you. Shame and guilt are often associated with traumatic events, and they don't belong in your life. You have the power of the button, to opt out of the torment of a traumatic event. It may be a part of your story, but it doesn't have to rule your life.

> **Once you are aware that a traumatic event has occurred in your life, you must now ask the question, Where is it?**

1. Can you recall a traumatic event that happened in your life?
2. Did this event throw you off course?
3. If yes, what did life look like before this happened?
4. If yes, what did this event teach you about yourself?
5. What emotions are associated with this event?

Chapter 6

YOU WILL MASTER IT

I've heard talk about children having the ability to adapt faster to situations than adults. This could be attributed to them not being set in their behaviors. Whether fact or fiction, resiliency is what we all need because adversity will come anyway. Howbeit true, this does not negate that some of life's pebbles can throw us off course, no matter how young or old the event in life is. As I have grown and begun to evaluate my life and others, I realize it's during infancy that we adopt less-than-authentic selves. This is because it's the stage we haven't mastered yet. We are mimicking and haven't built our confidence.

Our son was walking independently at nine months and loved to be in the bathroom shower to mimic what he saw us do. A little after he was a year old, we introduced the potty to his bathroom environment. Although my husband and I didn't apply pressure to potty training, we put a kid-size toilet in the bathroom so that he could become familiar and gravitate to it on his own, and he did. He took the initiative to sit on it without prompting, but he had not mastered it yet; in the process of time, I gave birth to a baby girl. As wonderful and blessed a life change as it was, it altered much in his life and ours. There was a new baby in the house, a mommy that was recuperating, and a very busy father that was assisting Mommy and doing the things that she would do in addition to his normal duties.

We changed our pattern, our schedule, our son's schedule, and made a major move across several states only a few weeks after the new baby was born. We moved into a foreign space, his potty that sat in the corner of the bathroom was not there and neither was his familiar house, friends, or school. After the dust settled from the transition, it seemed like we were starting over with the training, as there had been an interruption to his norm. Before this move, he was making great progress, but it was interrupted before he mastered it.

We had to put in work to acclimate him to a bigger thing called a toilet, because we didn't have access to his potty in this temporary space. The pebbles that came his way shifted him in his training and it seemed a little more difficult for potty-training; this was because there was now an expectation that he should know how to do it because he was older, was introduced to it already, and had been using his potty before. We had to take responsibility for the abrupt changes and create something that would work for all of us with the new variables. What may have seemed simple to us as parents was not as simple for him. EVERYTHING was new, so we had to be patient and be willing to teach and encourage him so that he could master this very necessary life skill. What I noticed is that he showed a different level of resistance because he was unfamiliar with much in this scenario. Sure, it would all pan out and this new home would become just as much home to him as the old one … but it would take time, because he was thrown some pebbles on the course before mastering the skill.

That is the hope of the adversary, that he could cause a level of disruption and agitation that will throw you off course in your early stages of development or recognition of purpose. The hope is that you never achieve, understand, or accept how valuable you are, how necessary you are, and how purposed you are by God.

> That is the hope of the adversary, that he could cause a level of disruption and agitation that will throw you off course in your early stages of development or recognition of purpose.

Therefore, here come the ITs! For all of us, this word bears different meanings and weight, but nonetheless, shareable emotions. Some of you barely made it out of the womb because your life scenario was less than perfect, or maybe outright crazy, at the point of inception.

See, I was not a planned or easily embraced pregnancy. My mother was an honor student on her way to college, with an option to graduate high school early. On her first time having sex, I was conceived. She had a very good home life and was depended on for much, as she was the eldest sister. There was disbelief that she could be pregnant because she was a home girl, but she'd chosen to entertain someone that kept moving. She also chose to forfeit her four-year college opportunity to keep a baby she did not know would change her life forever. She also faced doing it without the support of my father. Their interaction was once in life, only once. Can you imagine the level of pressure? Can you imagine the set of emotions or fears that tried to grip her?

Her mother was heavily into the church and she was noted as a stellar girl. From my understanding, although they were not excited, once they dealt with their emotions, they supported her in having the baby, and I am so glad. I am sure that this was a traumatic start, because it would change her life as she knew it. She had not mastered her teenage years but was moving to motherhood.

As I am writing this book, I am reflecting on a message that I heard Bishop Herbert Crump preach that penetrated my heart. It made me weep in service as it laid on my ears: "You did not make it through the fight in the womb to lose the battle on earth." This statement ricocheted in my spirit because this pebble, this fight, hit my pond of life at conception.

The very man that should have been able to embrace me, his seed, was the first to insert rejection. Not just because of his absence or inability to accept me, but the stories that I had to hear in later years of his blatant denial. The neighbor introduced my mom to his family. I had to hear stories that I was claimed as his "god-child" and there was different treatment from his family. This is what I mean about infancy. I had to come out of the gate swinging, fighting rejection.

I share this story not to shame my father, but to share the truth about seeds that we oftentimes don't realize we plant, or the tone that we set for relationships, or the fight that we inflict upon others—and many times on the people that we should love the most or are closest to. I understand he did what he could do for where he was in life. He moved at the level of his capacity, so for the first ten years of my life, Mama did it singly. We had a great support system and I had active male role models in my life. My uncles stepped up to the plate to teach my siblings and I things that a father would, but we were clear on who they were. For many, your story may be similar or subjectively worse; this is part of mine. This pebble thrown was not about my father; this was, again, a shot at my purpose.

The enemy got a glimpse of the greatness that God has woven in my life, and he wanted to get an early start on trying to convince me that I am not who God says I am. God had a plan mapped out and even this pebble was not a surprise to Him. The rejection or absence of my father was not a surprise to God, for He already gave the answer and resolution. He created me powerful, and He created me resilient. I formed in a womb of an undoubtedly scared teenage girl, who had the courage to keep going and keep fighting. We made it together in a healthy pregnancy and

I was able to endure the process of being alone in the womb: dark spaces, uncomfortable twists and turns, tight quarters, the breaking of water, and the pushes of delivery. I am born to WIN.

In your less-than-perfect scenario, with all the pebbles thrown on your path and all the life changes that you will experience, you must remember you are born for this and born ON PURPOSE. God was intentional about your survival in the womb, because you are equipped with all the tools you need to conquer evil on earth.

My son eventually adjusted to our new life. It took some coaching to help him get back on track with potty-training, but he got it and mastered it with all the changes; he mastered it, and so will you. He was influenced by what he saw us continually do. We are teaching, even when we aren't speaking.

There may be some areas in your life that you were doing good and then some life event occurred. You need to keep moving forward because you will get it. Regardless of what was thrown at you early in life, get up, dust off, regroup, and remember that you were born to win.

The interruption cannot be your stopping point. You still have a chance to master your skillset. You survived the pressure in the womb, and you will excel on earth.

1. Have you dropped something prior to mastering the skill?
2. What is it?
3. Why won't you return to it?
4. Do you recognize that you are a Winner?
5. Have you ever felt defeated?
6. In what areas have you WON?

Chapter 7

THE IT OF REJECTION

Rejection is something that all will experience in their lives; the degree to which it is experienced varies. Rejection is not intentional all the time, but that does not always take away the sting of it. It may occur at work, where you applied for a position and were overlooked, or you weren't accepted into the college of your choice, or you experience what seems to be favoritism of someone else in your family. It could be you never knew your biological parent, or you do, and he/she doesn't want to have a healthy relationship with you. Whatever the event or entry point, rejection is not a wonderful feeling, but I have heard a truth spoken by my husband, Jesse Stevenson, over the years: "Rejection changes your direction." If you are not accepted or embraced in one place, the closed door will cause to you have to move on to another place. Although many may see this as very negative, many times we are spared from greater damage when we are forced to move. The important point would be to process the pain and try to learn from the move.

Rejection is something that all will experience in their lives; the degree to which it is experienced varies.

Think for a moment when you were younger, in a relationship you described as the "love of your life." You thought the relationship was perfect for you, but your immaturity would not allow you to see the toxicity of it, and God allowed the relationship to fizzle out. Sure, you were hurt, you may have even been lonely; but in hindsight, you can see how this relationship would not have yielded you your best. So, then, this rejection was protection. A closed door protected you from what you didn't see.

The danger of rejection undealt with or unrealized can heighten self-rejection. A person can experience so many entry points of rejection that it can shape their mind to think that it is the acceptable norm and there is nothing better. Self-rejection causes one to settle, to have a distorted view of who he/she is, and can taint how a person sees others. It will never allow you to see your greatness, which is why IT must be identified and uprooted. This IT needs a termination notice in your life and emotions.

The fact that my father was the first man to reject me, I later realized in life that I wondered how another man would love me and if I would be good enough for him. After all, my father didn't want me. I can laugh at this pain now, but it wasn't funny then. I had formed a callousness toward men. I wanted a healthy relationship, I dreamed of being married early and having children, but God knew not to let me get married as early as I wanted to. I had not faced my IT of rejection and, in some ways, I didn't know that it was driving some of my behaviors. That is the danger of rejection. It can creep in and project in various behaviors and, if it is not traced deep enough, you may let it hang out unknowingly. And, like a weed alongside a plant, you allow it to choke out growth. I would be free in my interactions in environments that I felt safe or with people that I knew for a long time, but I was often more withdrawn in unfamiliar settings. I found that I was being stereotyped in my younger years. Some people stereotyped me for the fairness of my skin and physical appearance. Or, they said they thought I was "stuck up." I didn't know how to take these comments in because I was trying to survive. It probably had a lot to do with what I was carrying, even unknowingly. I was carrying the weight and pain of rejection even when it wasn't currently happening. There was only a portion of me on display, because much of my personality was hidden in layers of pain of past incidents. The root cause was the entry point of rejection from my father. The other layers came from the no's that I had received and awkward moments that I wouldn't fit into the circle or blatantly stand out. It took me a while to realize and accept that God was protecting me and the purpose for which He called me. Despite the rough start as a kid, I managed somehow to still have a big personality. Somehow, the pieces of me were big enough to shine through the clouds.

I had those in my life that embraced and cultivated my creativity, tenacity, and outgoing nature, and then there were those that did not know how to take such a personality from a young kid. I didn't fit the cookie-cutter-child mold, and many of you didn't either. There were a few family members that spoke suppressive words, and this was weighty, after having to deal with parental rejection to start. I realized some of the differences shown to me by family members was because I was not their "choice." I could feel much of this as a child, but as an adult I was able to identify it as rejection. I could name it. It was as if this entry point helped me to develop a discernment. Maybe this was one of the good things to come out of this scenario.

I kept going, but at some point, I had to go back and eject the negative words, the negative feelings—because, at later times, some of those words surfaced in my mind.

When we proceed over pebbles thrown in our ponds of life and emotions, we can proceed wounded or not be in the same level of strength as before. Sometimes you are not aware that what was said or done wounded you until you have an "aha" moment, or when something similar happens and reminds you of the pebble, and your reaction is for the old and the new. My hope is that you will be enlightened by the words on this page so that if you have an incident like this, you will be able to deal with it for what it is and not add old baggage. The baggage weighs you down and you have too much to accomplish to be limping and heavy with it. The pebble in the pond of your life does not have to ripple and continually keep you bound to something.

I was 17 when I began continuous and somewhat consistent relationship with my father. Although I knew who he was we did not talk much until I was 17. There were years of rocky moments; moments where we were teaching each other, but without him, I would not have been present. There were also years after trying to work on our relationship that we didn't speak, but confronting some of the issues helped us work out the kinks and be able to nurture a healthy relationship, while setting healthy boundaries. I had made up my mind that I would not allow this scenario to rule my life. I would not allow how our relationship began to be a determining factor of what it could become. I have a mother that loves hard and God blessed me with a phenomenal bonus dad, who has raised me since I was ten years old. I was the kid that asked questions, and they were willing to answer. My mother helped me to banish whispers in my life of untruths. I had many questions as to why my father wouldn't want me or to have a relationship with me. She helped me to silence the voice of parental rejection. The enemy wanted to taunt me with various scenarios surrounding my father and highlight the tumultuous moments, but I am so grateful that my mother never talked negatively about him. She allowed us to form our own relationship, at whatever point my father was willing to do so. Any opinion I had was not because she fed me toxic information. She put no effort into tearing him apart.

This was one of the first areas where I had to learn how to make healthy boundaries; not to badger or be badgered by what was, but make an intentional effort to create from where we were. Let's note here: it can be difficult to build a relationship with a young adult that has done it without you (the parent), but it is possible if you are in a good place and have the capacity to offer a healthy relationship. It will require respect on both sides, truthful conversations, time, and forgiveness—some vital things that can help one to get over and live past feelings of rejection. Today, my father and I have a respectable relationship and we are constantly building stronger bonds. I made a choice not to be bitter toward him; we both made a choice to put some time and effort into our relationship. Rejection is greater than someone not accepting you, it can make you doubt everything about yourself. Once you recognize that it has entered your life, you must process all of the associated feelings and eject it from your life.

1. What are some of your most challenging relationships?
2. What area in your life have you felt most rejected in?
3. What personality is agitated by your presence?
4. Do you realize that you are not the only one on the ship? Relationships are partnerships.
5. Are you happy with yourself?

Chapter 8

SUPPRESSION

You are created on purpose, so why would one stumble over answering questions about their purpose or gifts? Why can't you articulate what you are purposed to do? You were born in God's image, with dominion, power, and authority, so why can't you answer? You were fearfully and wonderfully made: you were given power, love, and a sound mind, why can't you articulate it? SUPPRESSION...Yes, natural gifts, abilities, talents, and desires suffer from suppression. We will discuss this so that you can be aware and not allow suppression to hide your gifts. You were created with vibrancy, and the mere fact that you made it out of the womb intact shows the level of power you possess. There were months of darkness and discomfort that came with your growth and development, but you were built to handle all of it.

Let's think about it for a moment. The egg grows into a fetus and endures coming through a birth canal or surgery (C-section) to be extracted, and you enter a room where there are giants.

Let's imagine for a moment: A brand-new baby born in a hospital that has never seen this world before and sees these giant hands, huge people, machines, noises—things that he/she has never seen or heard before. People are suctioning his/her nose (even though the baby has no clue what that is), someone is checking the heart, weight, and all the vital things to verify the baby's health. That must be a lot for a baby, but he/she quickly adapts. The baby will soon realize that it's safe and all is well; this is where the baby should be.

If as a baby you can make it through all these abrupt, swift changes, then surely as an adult you can get through anything. No one forced you to cry when you came out, not for food nor when soiled; it's in your ability to do so. Why then, when you are at a stage in your life that you can use words or are facing a great challenge would you not cry out for help? What would make you choose not to? Suppression can be a culprit...something, someone, or some event caused you to shut down a natural ability.

Some things you never questioned or dumbed down until someone made you second-guess yourself. It could have been harsh words that were supposed to be constructive, yet it was only criticism. Possibly the throw-offs and putdowns came from someone you trusted enough to lend your ear; whatever the entry point of suppression, it must be tracked. You were never created to sec-ond-guess yourself—that only happens when the voice, opinion, and persuasion of others is louder than your authentic voice.

> **Some things you never questioned or dumbed down until someone made you second-guess yourself.**

Too often, we don't go back and trace what occurred to take us out of character, what altered our ability to speak and communi-cate well. Some of the behaviors have been hidden for so long and been disguised as normal. They become accepted and are allowed to remain with us. We must check and trace the fruit produced from things that caused us to whimper or diminish.

If you stubbed your toe on a piece of furniture, you may find your-self apprehensive the next several times you walk by the furniture again because the trauma brings a memory. The apprehension is the reaction of the hurt, trying to avoid the same thing happening again. However, it is necessary to go back to that place of entry and confront the thing, so you can then walk straight, tall, and strong. The incident had you out of character and the memory can make you reactive. Surely, you survived the hurt; it may not have seemed like a big deal, but it threw you out of an original level of confidence.

Memories are real. They remind you of what has occurred, but I would encourage you to gain power over memories that caused trauma in your life. They are never to hold power over you, especially if you survived them. The memory should display how resilient you are; it should serve as a reminder that you faced the hand of the giant head-on and made it out alive. It should be a reference point of victory, not a tool of bondage. To rid the hard drive of your mind of painful memories, you must acknowledge what has occurred and eject it from your mind and your spirit, and not allow it to define who you are.

You must eject thoughts that fight against your progression, as well as thoughts that fight against your laughter.

It is noted that our brains produce as many as between 50,000 to 70,000 thoughts per day. (National Science Foundation/Huffington Post). It would be wise if you are ridding yourself of suppressive behaviors to be intentional and think about how many of those thoughts are replaying old, hurtful memories, as opposed to positive self-talk and edifying statements. Everything that God created was with a spoken word, but when you are compressed and weighed down, it's difficult to stand in good posture as well as clear speech. If we don't train our minds to think healthy, we will be weighed down and our joy will be depleted.

Suppression can also create a melancholy attitude, and if it sits too long, it may be difficult to trace its origin. You could be down in the dumps, but it has nothing to do with what's going on with you presently. It could be a damaging memory, emotion, or idea. Our minds have to be rid of negative emotions and thoughts that contradict our greatness and authenticity. When you experience suppression, you hold back on yourself and on your dreams. You could view a hill as a mountain and become less likely to take a leap.

You were born with giants in the hospital room, but it didn't stop you from crying out for help, and your cries had a certain assignment. You were built to overcome adversity; you were able to make your presence known in a crowded room. Your parent knew when "I'm wet," "I'm hungry," "I'm sleepy," "I don't feel well," because you were able to effectively communicate it.

You still possess that innate ability, but suppression has to be ejected from your mind and emotion-out of your life. As you rid yourself of old pain, you make room for progression, happiness and new memories.

All the pebbles thrown your way created a smokescreen from truth. Truth is what God spoke about you. Even if you fell off the wagon in life, you can't stay down. It is guilt, shame, and embarrassment that make you feel as if you can never stand tall in who you are, as though you deserve to be beat down and in a lowly place because of things that happened. Nevertheless, you must shift your mind and place it in a healthy place. The suppression must be traced and ejected!

> *"Finally, brethren, whatsoever things are true, whatsoever things are honest, whatsoever things are just, whatsoever things are of good report; if there be any virtue, and If there be any praise, think on these things."* (Philippians 4:8, KJV)

1. Can you remember a time when you didn't want to share your ideas and dreams?
2. Can you remember a time when you didn't want to speak?

3. Can you remember when you first struggled with your creativity?
4. Has anything diminished in your life? Has your laughter diminished? WHY?
5. What is an area in which you are holding back?
6. What makes you feel uptight or under pressure?
7. Do you feel an unhealthy pressure to perform?
8. Can you recall any negative words spoken in your life that may have halted or slowed your flow?
9. Were you ever told that you wouldn't be successful?
10. Were your compared negatively to a family member?
11. Did you have a teacher or mentor that taunted your dream?
12. Did you believe them?

Chapter 9

WHEN IT MAKES YOU MUTE

When life happens to you, IT can often stop you in your tracks. I have had a love for music as long as I can remember. I enjoyed being around music, listening to other people perform it, pushing myself and others in it. From childhood, I sang and wrote music frequently, until one day I found myself feeling like I couldn't do either. I knew that it was a feeling because in previous times, if I couldn't do anything else, I could do music. I had to wonder how I reached this feeling. What happened in my life?

I also recall a time where I didn't want to hear music while riding down the road, because my headspace was crowded and I needed quiet time. I had so many thoughts to process. I am a thinker, so quiet time is very important to me. In my reflective time, I realized that I was pushing parts of me to the background.

As I have been encouraging you in this book to trace back, my search led me to the word change . The recent changes that had occurred in my life moved me to a block of abnormal silence in my music life. I had faced some physical challenges with my pregnancy and it caused me to stop working, so I lost my social network on my job. While I was already out of work, there was talk about a possible out-of-state family move for us, but with no firm information on it. It was a sensitive time in our lives, but we knew that we had to make moves; we just weren't sure of what we were to do. When the baby was a few weeks old, we received a clear answer but there was not much time to maneuver. You can imagine the level of pressure; this was not an ideal scenario. I had just had my second C-section in two years and had to start packing up our house to move. I would have preferred to spend my time just recuperating. Let me insert here: this was not my first time making a major move. I had done it three times already across several states and the first two times I did alone. However, now the circumstances were different. In times past, I knew I was leaving with a new personal opportunity and career move.

This time, I was leaving the place that had been home to me for the past five years, leaving my career behind without answers to the next step: a new baby, moving out of one home and not certain of the next. The home that we were looking to purchase was taken off the market two weeks prior to our move date. To add to all these dynamics, I had only visited this new place twice and had not built any relationships with others. If I had looked at this at face value and all the rocky moments that presented themselves, I would have missed the truth about what God spoke regarding this move for our family. I would have made facts larger than my truth.

The relocation and challenges of change affected my voice, literally. When I first moved, I was hoarse often, which is something that I never dealt with on a regular basis in the past. To add to the bucket, I wasn't using my voice much. Normally, I was always vocally active. I had just left a place where I was facilitating services, singing at events, singing at church and in my private time, to relocate to a place where I would sit during service and no community involvement. This was a big contrast. While dealing with the hoarseness, I necessarily had to sing much less. This change hit my confidence for singing, because I could not produce what I normally would. All this bothered me, but I wasn't sure what to do.

One day, it came to me that I did not have a right to stop singing. My voice has a sound that is needed on the earth. In a place where I once felt confident, I began to feel challenged, apprehensive, and timid. Those were not words used to describe me because that is not who I am. I worked to get to the bottom of IT. What in the world was making me feel like this? Why would I second-guess myself in an area that I was born to be in?

The original melodies that would just flow out of me seemed blocked. The sound of my voice was different, and I wasn't sure how to process or use it. Baby hormones, geographical changes, and the social isolation was influencing me. I realized and knew that I had to work through it and overcome it.

> **The original melodies that would just flow out of me seemed blocked.**

The more I talked to God about it, the more He gave me information. I had to take an introspective look at this matter and saw that it stretched beyond these particular changes. I had to kill the spirit of comparison—within myself. I was looking for some things to be as they were.

Of course, that wouldn't be true for my geographical location, or my home, or the obvious life changes, but I was looking for my voice to be something that I could recognize.

The fact that I had a baby before and didn't experience these changes made them new for me. But I was expecting to do what I normally could, and it wasn't happening. In my assessment, I had to be honest with myself about the fact that I wasn't using my voice as much; I had shrunk there. In this new place, most people had no idea that I even sang. I am certain my social and emotional island influenced my desire to sing. Everything about life was different and I felt vulnerable on various levels. I was looking for a solution, because I had not adjusted to my change.

As I was dealing with challenges with my voice and shrinking in my gift, I realized there were many singers that I knew had been on pause, on mute as well. They didn't have the desire to sing with or in front of anyone. Skill was not their issue, but a life IT was. They didn't give up on God, but life happened. For some it was distrust, and if there is any place where we want to uproot an IT, it's in the trust area. Distrust can affect every area of our lives, causing us to miss out on valuable things and opportunities. God uses our relationships with others in varying degrees as we build so it's imperative that we are able to trust.

I have had conversations with several worshippers that said, "I just want to come to church and worship; I don't want to deal with all the drama." I had some declare the lack of desire to sing because of things that they had seen and experienced: bad business deals, public mistakes, inconsistent opportunities, crab in the bucket mentality, etc. Some of the singers and musicians alike felt that people were more in love with the gift in them and not concerned about their person, and it caused pain and withdrawal within them.

Some of their situations were different than mine, but we were all facing being mute. Some of us were trying to get back on the wagon and some were just in limbo and denial.

Because I was personally facing this, it was easier for me to see the despair of others in this area. I had levels of sensitivity, compassion, and knowledge that I didn't have before. I was concerned about me and so many other people that were facing this mountain, and I wanted to encourage us to move forward. Here again, purpose was pushing forward in my challenge. I am an exhorter of potential; it's a part of who I am!

I knew I had to fight to get through this and come out on top. I made intentional decisions and set a reminder in my phone every day titled "sing." During this time, I reflected on the things that God spoke to me about my life: the writing, the singing, the ministry gift that I was able to share with various people. My voice is like no one else's, but I realized that there was a sphere of influence that God gave me. There were people that connected with my voice. There were people that preferred to hear me. I thought about how words that come out of my mouth have power and are effective. So, if I gave in to the pressure to become mute, someone may be hanging in limbo. I did not, and do not, want to have anyone in limbo because I was out of place.

I would sing at that phone reminder, and when prompted, I would record and send it to various people. They had no idea of the timidity that tried to come upon me. They didn't know what I was working through, but they were a no-judgment zone. They didn't hear my flaws or make comparisons to what I was making comparisons with. I got responses like "I needed this today," "Thank you for sending this," "I love your voice." I was building myself back up and confronting my IT—when the worshipper couldn't sing.

It is a challenging spot when the worshipper can't sing, because so much is conveyed for me in those moments. The enemy wanted to make me stale. If I continually avoided that time of transparency and intimacy via worship, it would keep those melodies blocked.

There are some things that are voice-activated and in my "norm," I would pour my emotions into my singing. It was worship to Him, while it was an outlet and cleansing for me. I could be free in my singing or writing, simply uninhibited. So, this challenge was about much more than the song. This was about my life, my existence in authenticity.

Not everyone is graced with the gifts that you possess. You were chosen for a specific reason; you do not have the right to quit and go mute. You can enhance, grow, sharpen, and add to yourself, but you are not called to fear and timidity. You are not created for those. You learn them … and that is why you must eject them.

I remember years before when I was building a new home. It was stressful for me, a single woman. I was doing something that many in my family had never done before. I was not in my native city, so I couldn't bounce things off Dad, Mom, or family members I trusted to help me make choices. I would go into the shell of the house as it was being erected and sing. I have never experienced anything like that since. New songs would come, new melodies and fresh sounds. The house went up with worship in the foundation. I prayed for the builders, I prayed for all involved, and I pressed through the process and completed it.

There were challenges, delays, and a few minor setbacks as weather and such affected the build. I had to draw on these memories during my current transition to help me fight and not go on mute. I reminded myself of those days that I would press pass the delays and stay in the shell of the home. When I didn't yet see the finished construction of the house, I knew that it was coming; it would soon be done.

I saw and lived in the finished product, but it was my faith that helped me through the middle. The notes resonating in my spirit helped me to deal with all the changes. I learned in the home-building scenario not to look at my opposition only as "What did I do wrong?", but rather, "Can God trust me with this job?"

We all have a measure of faith, but some of us are more gifted in it; this is when you may feel like you are constantly having to push through life and use lots of muscle. Your faith is being built and your sound defined. You must not allow your trials, challenges, or pebbles thrown at you to reduce your sound, because your sound will help to ensure your victory. Your sound has a frequency that will penetrate. Your sound is distinct and powerful.

Now that I'd endured the construction, shortly after moving in, God began to do some things in me that required another change. I had to streamline my life pattern. I had to streamline what I was involved in at church, and I came off the social scene in ways that were normal for me. It was challenging because I enjoyed hosting things at my home; I was involved in various departments at church, but I recognized that God was sharpening another area of my life and another skillset.

I began to write more than I ever had, much more than songs, as my ears were being tuned to hear from God in a way that I had not before—but it did require me to pull away. I remember one day my friend called and asked me to go out and I had to decline. She asked, "Are you still in isolation?" We chuckled, but she respected my process. I did not understand it then, but I am so glad that I stuck to the "isolation" because years later, it helped me in unfamiliar territory. God had me practice in a place where I was well-connected and loved for what was to come years later. If I had not faced those moments then as a single woman in an empty house, I don't know how much strength I would have gathered to face the isolated place post-partum with a family. The awesome thing about God is that He will increase you, prepare you, and has created you to win. I had to draw on that strength from years past to help me face the present obstacle. I literally had to draw on my previous victory to increase my faith in the new moment.

Knowing who I am, although not liking some of these variables, helped me to stand with confidence that I would make it through, but it also caused me to dig deeper into myself.

I learned about processes in the waiting, while I increased in strength and temperance. I faced the building of the home even with the overwhelming pressure, uncertainties, and being out of my comfort zone. The memory of this home-building experience reminded me eight years later that I could thrive in this new move, with this new house, in another place of "isolation." It was the previous victory that I could draw on and know, with assurance, if He brought me through, then He would do it again. So, I kept singing, even when I didn't like to hear myself. I kept singing and I began to feel the songs, hear them, and write them. The songs were there: I had to get over it—the IT that came to make me mute.

Years later, that experience of building a new home was helping me in a new season of life. God was setting me in place to see progression and more of Him. This move was not a surprise to God, and He knew I would have to leave that career. It was a vulnerable space for me.

Interestingly, I wanted to leave my career years before, and my husband told me that the time was not yet here; I had to wait. When the time came, it didn't look anything like I'd hoped.

One place of opposition helped me to be prepared for the next. The songs that I laid out in the atmosphere years ago were stored for me when I couldn't articulate any new words.

You cannot give in to the pressure of what is going on around you and become mute. With intention, you must speak God's word of promise into every matter in your life. We don't always understand our process but we know that all of the puzzled pieces must come together and work out for our good-it's a promise. Challenges will come and you may feel like shutting down, but you can't. If we view the pebbles wrongly, our perspectives will be off. If there is a ripple in the water, you can choose to relax or fight against the current. However, keeping your ears tuned and praise on your lips will help you to know the difference. The songs will lift your spirit as you wait, provide peace as the waves are crashing around you, and encourage someone else that is watching your process. You are born to win; it's *your* pond, don't be mute. You have authority to speak life into yourself and others daily. You must speak and sing, even when you may not want to hear yourself. Your voice has power and a sphere of influence.

1. Have you ever felt mute?
2. Can you identify where this feeling originated?
3. Can you remember a scenario that made you feel vulnerable enough shut down?
4. Are you willing to fight for your voice?

Chapter 10

THE STRUGGLE AFTER THE WOUND

When the IT in your life causes you to struggle with love, it's time to face it and deal with the wound. The IT in your life can cause you to struggle with authentic relationships and push away those that love you, leaving you questioning if you can have it—LOVE. The wound in your life can leave you not knowing how to fully receive it, making you believe it's too good to be true. When we are wounded, doubt and fear tend to highlight the area of failure or pain in us. It is necessary to heal from things so that wounds won't define our lives.

Our ability to love is natural; we only form a callousness when we are injured or there is something that causes us to lose hope in love. An IT in your life can allow tolerance for unhealthy relationships, because a wounded area of your heart can reduce your expectation of better.

Without realizing it, this loss of hope can create self-inflicted isolation and a hardening of your gentle nature, or it can cause you to inflict pain on others. I was recently talking to some ladies and the topic of love and relationships surfaced. There was an obvious shift in their demeanor. One of the women was now suffering with self-inflicted abusive behavior because of her wounded space, and she openly voiced her disdain for men and their lack of commitment to relationships. Her wound created a desire for her to never be out of control, to seek out men younger than her, so that

63

she could "use" them and keep going. It was a consensus in the room among these particular individuals, most of whom had been abused in some form or another. The abusers were people that they should have been in healthy relationships with, as opposed to total strangers. They were wounded and now struggling to love themselves and others.

No one wants to be wounded, and certainly not repeatedly; but if it happens, what can you do to live beyond it and not recreate the pain that was inflicted upon you? There must be a realization of what has occurred in your life and a process of forgiveness and healing. The lack of either holds you prisoner. Your energy that should be used to build can turn into destructive behavior, and sometimes the offender has moved on and left you STUCC—Still Tackling Unresolved Cognitive Clutter.

If identification and realization of a wound does not occur, it will be difficult to experience healing and impossible to experience wholeness.

I am married now, but there was a point in my life when I wondered if it would ever happen. As a young girl, I wanted to be married at eighteen. It was well after that when it happened for me. I had set an expectation for what I thought was a good idea. Let me just insert here that I am so happy that God did not answer that prayer. The desire came from me being a nurturer and having a loving family. I am the eldest of my mother's children and have always been known to be a "momma." Nevertheless, with the pebbles that had been thrown in my pond, I would have been ill-prepared to be a parent or wife, especially at the age of eighteen.

I was certainly one that was pushing away love. As friendly, outgoing, socially aware, and involved as I was, I had a guarded heart. I tried puppy love, but it wasn't working for me. Over the years, I met nice men with great careers and overall nice personalities, but I was tough. The crazy thing about the toughness is, if you made it past the wall, I was all in. The trick was to get past the wall. I realized that I was keeping things and people out. I came to a point where I was intentional about spending time with myself and addressing things so that I could learn how to convey the matters of my heart to others. One of the prayers I began to pray was, "Lord, please give me singleness of heart. Any matter, person, offense that I have experienced, help me to release it." I will admit that this was not an easy process because there were many times I wondered what was wrong with me, why I was always the brides-maid and showing up to all these family events alone. Well ... again, I am so thankful that God loves me enough that He allowed me to confront myself and the things that I had experienced, which caused me to morph into this space. I am clear that this was not His original idea for me—rather, I had taken on a non-authentic personality when it came to love.

I heard others say things like, "You can't just marry anybody," "You can't settle," "God has a special mate for you" – but none of these felt good at the time; they were encouraging but didn't feel good.

To be honest, there were some moments on this path that caused me to want to just do things my way. "If I am waiting, praying and hoping for a GOD mate and he still hasn't come, I may as well do what I want." This is not a wise decision. If you are reading this book and are in that space, dismiss it. It will bring you unnecessary heartache and you still will have to wait. Even if you are struggling to love, you do not want to fall in love in the wrong place or with the wrong person.

I reflect on confronting areas of my life and how shortly there-after I met the person that I would later marry. Had I not done the excavation; we would have clashed when we met. The months of exposing my vulnerable areas prior to meeting him helped me to be able to receive the idea of friendship.

Once I realized that there were layers to what I was dealing with, I begin to address the wounds. Any wound should have a min-imal amount of attention paid to it, but depending on the depth and severity of the wounded area of your heart, drastic measures must be taken.

IT must be washed, cleansed, and treated, so that it has a fair chance at healing and not spread to other areas.

> **Any wound should have a minimal amount of attention paid to it, but depending on the depth and severity of the wounded area of your heart, drastic measures must be taken**

In my healthcare career, I treated many patients that had circulatory issues and some of those lead to wounds—varying degrees, sizes, and treatments. The physicians, nurses, and technicians paid close attention and took these wounds seriously. We were taught to exhibit high standards of sanitization and cleanliness before, during, and after treating patients, because not doing so could cause infection and increased complications. Bandages had to be changed during wound care treatment, sometimes debridement was necessary, cutting away at the infection, packing some with medical gauze, and washing them with sterile rinses. The wounds could not be ignored; if they were and went untreated for too long, necrosis (tissue death) could occur. The infection could literally cause other working limbs and parts to be affected. The same can happen to us if we leave wounded areas of our lives unattended. One of the biggest fallacies is "Ignore it; it'll go away." Well, if it's bleeding, it will mess up your garments and begin to smell. If we need help, we must get it.

There is a tool in this world of wound care called a wound vac. This tool is attached to the wound and does a suctioning motion with a canister attached, extracting the infection out of the wound. This is a drastic step in the effort to give the wound a chance to heal and keep circulation going. The infection is visible in the canister, but it is contained. The person treating a wound is on a regimented, weekly schedule to ensure that all work is productive, because the goal is to heal.

For those that leave the wounds alone longer, it may require a surgical procedure that may or may not be successful. There is a greater chance of healing if the wound is not allowed to get out of control.

Because our emotional wounds are not visible, they can be easier to push past if we "act" as if they never occurred. Some wounds can be contained while others will fester. If we allow wounds to fester, they can create systemic issues and cause our lives to smell. The sweet fragrance that we should emit will be covered by toxic infection instead. In the natural world, it's difficult to ignore a wound indefinitely because it's painful and visible, but mentally it can be easy to cover it up. Either way, our progress is affected. When we are wounded, our minds realize that an injury has happened. We experience the pain physically and emotion-ally. However, if we persist in pushing past the pain, we smother an authentic portion of ourselves.

We are to be and function as God's original design, not the make-up and costumes that we apply. You must pay attention to the types of behaviors you develop after being wounded. Sometimes the behaviors cause you to be withdrawn, diminish your creativity, and/or lose your smile or laughter: but none of these things are the original design of who God created you to be, as they shifted only after the wound occurred. They are symptoms that must be treated and healed. As with a physical wound, we must be willing to attach an "emotional" wound vac to extract all of the toxins and infections in our emotions so that we can heal.

Some of the behaviors that we have learned to embrace as part of survival must be ejected from our lives. Behavior modification is necessary after we have been wounded. For example, someone breaks your trust and you realize it's happened; you put up a wall, and you change your natural ability to interact with people because you want to avoid a repeat of the pain. No one wants to have their trust broken, but we also can't walk around with walls erected. The wall that you built up became part of you because you felt it was what you needed to protect yourself, but what did you keep out by having that wall up? What did you not experience in fullness because the symptom of distrust was not dismissed by you? Who did you stifle?

Depending on the nature of your wound, you must develop a treatment plan; things must be shifted to save your life. Do you need to delete phone numbers? Do you need to change your circle of friends as you strengthen and heal? Do you need to guard your ears? What healthy boundaries can you put in place for an effective treatment plan?

If you had an incision to your body, you may experience bruising, nerve pain, itching, and various reactions that are an indication that something happened, and something is healing. You cannot act like nothing happened, but you must allow the process of healing to take place in its proper time for the nature and severity of your wound. It's tempting to get up and move too fast if you can walk with a crutch, or if you have on a boot, or if you are walking with a limp, but it does not mean you are at full capacity yet. When a pebble in your pond has been thrown at your ability to love, it will affect everything about you as well. It will affect what you produce and how well you advance.

It's easy to apply make-up in such a seductive culture. And in this context, I certainly don't mean tangible make-up. Some of us are emotionally made-up. We have subscribed to the "fake it till' you make it" theory. Although I understand part of that concept is to keep moving forward, I have seen many get stuck at the faking part. If you fake long enough, you can believe your own lies, as opposed to confronting your wounded area. You can begin to make up stories, make up lifestyles, make up personalities that diminish the reality of what has occurred and who you presently are or were created to be. Being made up can cause you to lose sight of what you are made of and when you see authenticity and true love, you push it away.

The wound can cause a callousness to come over you, which warps perception and causes cognitive distortions. The fact that you were wounded can create the expectation that this pain is what you deserve. But you must treat the wound to be able to experience true healing. We are rooted and grounded in love: love covers, love heals, and love encourages, so you can't give up on love or push it away. You must love larger than you did before you ever were wounded. Challenging, YES...but what's your alternative?

Are you willing to allow a pebble to steal your greatness and life? Hopefully you are not. So you learn to love and discern authentic, healthy, partnership-relationships. The ship is never just about you alone; it takes people and their skills to operate this world, so you can't live and function in it alone. You deserve good, healthy love.

You must remember that some of the pebbles you encountered were from people that had been injured themselves and they could only give you what they have -unresolved wounds. So, it's extremely important for you to heal so that you will not recycle what was inflicted upon you. It may be a struggle not to hurt others because it was done to you, but we must choose not to be prisoners to the pains of our past.

How you love can be determined by the love that was given to you, but we all must ask God how to love based on the capacity that He gave us as individuals.

You were created to love and live in dominion, authority, and power. The symptoms, left untreated, can diminish your power to love, to be sensitive and compassionate. You will miss out on an intended purpose for your life if you don't heal completely.

Sometimes we recognize and can admit the damage that has happened in our lives. You can admit that you were rejected, violated, abused, and/or abandoned: but do you recognize the adverse effects that have taken place in your life from the entry point of your wound?

The symptoms of wounds can make subtle entries into the fabric of our beings, when we just keep moving and do not take time to evaluate why we function the way that we do. This is how dysfunction is shared from one generation to the next; no thought is given to your movements, just that you move. We must be intentional about what we do, as being intentional will have you evaluate your values and principles. If you are on autopilot, you may not have realized that what you're doing is outdated, causing you to expel more energy or experience exhaustion. Instead, you can stop, regroup, evaluate, and relaunch yourself. Sometimes what worked five years ago needs fine-tuning or complete dismissal from our lives, but it requires us to have an intentional awareness of what we are doing and why in order to change.

Sometimes our perspective is off as we experience trials and are wounded because of the pain of those trials. We must bring that pain into proper alignment and make a conscious effort to be better and constantly grow apart from the pain. If you were rejected in one relationship but heal and learn what you need from it, it won't define all of your relationships. However, if you think that all people are alike, your pain helps you to create and expectation of failure regarding your future relationships. We don't want to become complacent in our efforts to live happy and healthy in our relationships, we must be intentional to heal. When we fight with love, it can create a callousness and that can cause numbness and a lack of direction in our lives. We fight our emotions when we feel them, because feeling brings a memory of pain. Struggling with a bad memory can cause you to miss a present moment and opportunity to create new, healthy memories. When not processed and ejected that memory now has freedom to control your life, opposed to just being a mere point of awareness.

> ## Sometimes our perspective is off as we experience trials

Have you found yourself in the space of stubbornness in your emotions, thinking, "That's just the way that I am used to doing things?" Are you evolving? Are you maximizing? Are you growing? This statement above ("That's just the way that I am") can be dangerous to our growth and development because it shuts out being open to new, innovative, and creative ideas. It shuts down our ability to welcome love. When we are operating in a calloused place, we shut out fresh things. If we are honest, there are some things in our lives that we survived but may not have been the best for us. You must question whether these scenarios caused you to experience adverse effects afterward.

Those adverse effects can shape how you view love, relationships, and people. Some things should not be repeated and should be dismissed.

Without conscious evaluation of our actions after being wounded, we could be moving and working but not experiencing quality productivity. We are called to produce good fruit, so you must prune the areas that were traumatized and get back into the flow as it was prior to your wound—your authentic flow. The refusal to stop and reset yourself can affect all that you are involved in.

Love covers all and love will heal every wounded space. You cannot carry your capacity to love fully with an unhealed area. You can't walk the same distance while wounded. Love yourself enough to cut away at any sickness that will keep you in bondage; you were born in love—to love.

I can relate to the callous because I was once the tough, young lady that went back and faced my distrust, failure, and disappointment in myself, and others, when it came to love. I wrote about it, cried about it, forgave, and let go. I had an intense writing session one day in my house and wrote a piece that freed me. A few weeks later, I met the man that I would marry. I had no idea of this when I met him, but God knew it. I can say that my husband met a woman that no man in my life ever had. The walls that were automatically erected and had to be chiseled down were no longer there, which was something new for me. I still had to learn who this girl was and fall in love with her but I had made much progress.

When we knew that marriage was in our future, he did the honorable thing and asked my father for my hand. Dad said, "I was wondering what took you so long—I knew you were the one when she wanted us to meet you, because I never had to run any man away before; she did a good job at that."

I told you I was tough, but real love, God's love for me, erased the wound and made me want to trust again. Even in the vulnerable areas that I had to share with my future husband, as we got to know each other, I was willing to share them because my hope was restored. I was willing to love. The IT that caused me to struggle with love was conquered by love. I wasn't expected to be perfect; God sent the person that would accept me, and I was intentional on loving again. LOVE wins every time.

1. What is an area in your life that makes you angry or causes irritability?
2. Have you forgiven those that hurt you?
3. Have you forgiven yourself for hurting others?
4. Have you recognized the entry point in your life that made you not love to the fullest?
5. How will you wash and cleanse the wound of your heart?
6. What intentional actions will you take to be FREE?
7. What treatment plan will you put in place to heal?
8. What is the frequency of your plan? Repeat until healed.

Chapter 11

WHAT'S SAID CAN HELP TO FRAME YOU

Whether you speak to those walking by or simply stare at them can be affected by where you were raised and cultured. As I walked down the sidewalk in the suburban streets of upstate New York, it's not the hustle and noise of the city or beeping horns but rather the breeze and the chirping of birds I hear. A quick look up and then away is common, but not the exchange of words with a stranger. There have been salutations that have left my mouth with no return; it's just the way it is. In contrast, to the south, it's totally normal to speak to and hold conversations with absolute strangers, wave at the cars passing by, and honk in a gentle manner to those sitting on a porch. As a generalization, northerners will look you in the eye and keep going, but southerners find this a bit abnormal. Both behaviors have been woven into the culture and deemed acceptable, but the truth is that both people have the capacity to speak and acknowledge each other's presence, regardless of where they have been raised or live. It becomes a decision to go with what's common.

It's the same as with the words that are spoken to you or the ones you speak. Whether the words are positive or negative, they can infiltrate your psyche and frame your life views, concepts, and ideas. It becomes a decision to hold on to the influence of them once you have a meter to determine what's best.

Many people travel the world to experience various cultures and move from their native states to new ones. My family and I are southerners that relocated to the north. It is always interesting to get some of the responses we do. Just the other day, my hubby and I were shopping in the office supply store. The manager was assisting us but was needed by another associate for the gentleman behind us. The manager asked us if he could help him quickly. We agreed, and he ran off to get what was needed. That left us at the counter with the other customer, so as we waited, I turned and said, "Hello there, how are you today?" Kindly, he answered, "I had a real rough day, but I'm okay," and he began to share some of the details of his challenging day. We shared a few words of encouragement and I turned back around. The gentleman then said to me, "Where are you from?" I chuckled and said, "Why, don't I sound like I am from New York?" He said "No, but the accent is not why I asked; it was the fact that you asked me how I was doing—New Yorkers don't do that." This interaction led to a full conversation between the three of us. But it also made me think about the fact that you don't have to subscribe solely to what you have been exposed to of behavior, be it good or bad. He was holding a conversation with me, a total stranger, and is a native New Yorker. Although he didn't initiate it, we shared some good conversation and he and Jesse, my husband, exchanged numbers. It was good ole southern charm, right here in New York.

Regardless of how you were taught to speak or respond, you can operate in the nature that God intended. You are capable of change. Why would it be such a difference from one state to the next when we are in the same country? It's exposure!

Is it wrong from one place to the next? No, it is common because it is culture. Once we learn to respect others amid our diversities, we can find common ground or at least respect for our human natures.

I am sure that you have had experiences in your life that you may have been pressured by because of your surroundings, but I want to talk about words spoken to you and the power that they possess, and how you can be influenced by them.

One of the biggest lies told is, "Sticks and stones may break my bones, but WORDS NEVER HURT!"

We must be responsible with words and use them for edification. When we talk about an IT in our lives, we must think about what was spoken to us, and how it shaped our thoughts about ourselves, others, and the world in which we live in. Although it is true that God made you in His image, in the likeness of Him, we came through a natural birth process and we don't get to choose the family we were born into. What we say about our lives, the lives that we carry spiritually and naturally, can have a great effect on them. Some of us had to fight words, words that were spoken negatively about our futures and destinies.

Words hold power, but you can counteract the concentration of negativity in your life when you speak words of life, when you practice healthy communication and declarations over your life and others.

I once heard someone say, "When you don't have much, you will take anything." That really got me to thinking. It is so important for us to know who we are and our value because we are not made to settle. If the power of negative words have beaten you down, I want to let you know that you possess the capacity to stand up again. Some things that we have accepted as normal must be dismissed from our thought patterns and our speech. You must fortify your mind with healthy thoughts so that those words can come from your mouth. You will be willing to speak healthy, as you think healthy.

I was holding a conversation with a young girl and she said to me, "If you hear certain things long enough, you will start to believe them." In this conversation, I had to ask her to think about what she had heard, because her situation presented something opposite to what was being said to her. The adverse words were trying to gain control over her mind. What she had heard was a lie, but it didn't stop the fight in her mind from those words.

In a bit of a contrast, there is another story that I particularly want to share with you. I had the opportunity to sit with a young woman that had been married and divorced, on drugs and clean, but found herself in a cycle. She was facing the reality of some of her adverse moments. When she opened up to me, she told me that she was sure she didn't want her kids to be like her, but when I asked her who she was, she struggled to answer me. I asked again, "Who are you?" Much of her answer she had to dig far back for because she was defining herself based on her present state, as opposed to her purposed self. Her truth was all these labels: divorcee, convict, addict, prostitute, but I was asking her to see herself beyond these titles. If she could see and define herself with her purpose, then we could put a goal in place to pursue. One of the challenges in her seeing herself was the words that had sat so deep in her spirit. She told me that she and her efforts were never good enough. One of her family members verbalized this to her frequently and she begin to believe the words spoken. As a child, she was involved in activities, sports, took vacations, and partici-pated in all types of extracurricular activities, but what stood out, loud, amid the positive experiences were the negative words from others. These words penetrated her spirit and began to manifest in behaviors that were contrary to her God design.

As she got out of her parents' house, she married a man that made her feel the same way, telling her, again, she wasn't good enough. As she began to get into trouble, she heard it from the officers around her. Her eyes filled with tears as I asked her to go to the recesses of her mind from before that belief came about. "What do you like to do? What are your hobbies? What are your gifts? If you could choose a career, who would you be?" When she redirected her thoughts, I was speaking to a hardworking, loyal, honest, nurturing nurse. And that is how I addressed her, not by her errors and flaws. There was so much her kids could aspire to be like ... in HER. The words had her in limbo, but the choice to speak life now has her words redirecting her self-image.

There are some limitations that may have been spoken over you, declarations of what you would not achieve or be—those are lies, but nevertheless, they have caused a fight. It's a fight that does not have to defeat you.

The enemy of your destiny would tell you that because you were born to a certain family, lived in a certain neighborhood, or attended a certain school, you wouldn't amount to greatness: those are lies. Some of those words could have been about your height, weight, skin tone, or race, but those are not the determining factors of your success. Some of those words could have been spoken because you didn't achieve what other family members had or didn't follow in their footsteps. If you live in an environment that fosters your greatness, then you create an expectation and practice of greatness. If you live in an environment that constantly tells you that you can't achieve greatness, without any counteraction to it, you may believe it.

> **If you live in an environment that fosters your greatness, then you create an expectation and practice of greatness**

It may be one person that sees your greatness and can grow it, regardless of how much negativity you hear. I want for all of us again to consider that the voice of man shall not be louder than the voice of God in our lives. We don't want to try to prove who we are based on cultural standards, but we should know and have definition by what God has spoken and purposed for our lives. Our attitudes and behaviors should not yield to the pressures of what society says. Your thoughts and speech cannot be confined to what you see.

You must be able to articulate your purpose, gifts, skills, and abilities. You must be able to speak what you desire and set healthy boundaries in place for your life. It does not matter where you began, but you must know where you are going. If you are sure about one thing, you must put your words on it and frame your world with your words. There are many things that you cannot choose. However, framing your world with your words is something you must make a priority to do.

If you are told you can't do something, you must know when you can and call into place the tools that you need to get it done. You must place energy and effort into your speech.

There will always be an opportunity for you to doubt yourself, but it is a costly one that you cannot afford. Make it a daily plan to speak positive affirmations over all that concerns your life. The negative words spoken were failed attempts on your purpose. But now that you know it was a tool meant for your demise, take the face off the attack and deal with the spirit of negativity. Build and sharpen yourself with positive talk, affirmations, and declarations that will shape your world. Make the choice that even when others have spoken negatively, you won't join the culture but will create a positive one wherever you have been planted, because you have the capacity to do so.

1. I am successful.
2. I am disciplined.
3. I am focused.
4. I am enough!
5. I am empowered to prosper.
6. I have what I need to overcome.
7. I am victorious.
8. I have courage.
9. I will retain the information that is presented to me.
10. I will build and nurture healthy relationships.
11. I operate with a clean heart.
12. I am free in my mind, body, and spirit.
13. I live a stress-free life.

14. My thoughts are pure.
15. I am rooted and grounded in love.
16. I forgive those that have hurt me and those that I have hurt. I forgive myself; I am free from bondage inflicted upon me and that which I accepted.
17. I like who I see in the mirror.

Create your list and be intentional to speak. Change your list but remain intentional.

Chapter 12

WHEN IT CAUSES YOU TO FIGHT

The trauma and crises that you experience in your life can inter-rupt your path, but also cause a fight on the inside of you. We mentioned earlier about coming out of the womb fighting. As I thought about this, the Bible story of Jacob and Esau would serve as a primary example of such; a fight in the family between twin brothers. Jacob was holding on to Esau's heel as he came out of the womb. (Genesis 25:26, KJV) He fought for Esau's birthright and used trickery to get the blessing from his father Isaac. Neither of the brothers signed up for this but it was the brother's situation. One of the interesting things that I found among the layers of this story was when Isaac said these words to Esau:

> *"You will have to fight to live, and you will be a slave to your brother. But when you fight to be free, you will break away from his control."*
> *(Genesis 27:40, ERV)*

This spoke volumes to me because there was much for Esau to be disgruntled about. The blessings that were to be pronounced over him was stripped because of family trickery and deception. Although his father could not change the fact that he spoke bless-ings over Jacob instead of Esau, he offered him strategy to freedom. There are realities that you and I both face, with some we did not ask or sign up for. There are some things that you may feel like you missed out on, or just an internal fight that is happening because of decisions made for you and some of your own. Whatever the case, however grim the reality is, there is a truth that remains: When you recognize what it is that aims to control you and your authentic person, you have power to experience true freedom because you are aware of the culprit. When you recognize what has caused an inner fight then you are able to confront and stop the cycles that desire to throw you off kilter. You will be able to identify what you were fighting but more importantly getting yourself on track to run after purpose. You will be able to break away from its control-whatever that has tried to enslave you. Obtaining freedom from the inner fight- whether through prayer, therapy or counseling- will cause you to receive what God has assigned and promised you. Once you are aware, you may see missed opportunities but don't focus on missed opportunities, realize what you have, and move forward.

There was a point, after years had passed and geographical locations had changed, when Esau was no longer angry with Jacob, he was able to tell Jacob to keep his peace offerings because he had multiplied so much. Esau said to Jacob "Oh Brother, I have plenty of everything-keep what is yours for yourself." Genesis 33:9 (Message bible).

Esau had healed, he no longer wanted to put energy into what Jacob did because GOD still blessed Esau. He was able to forgive Jacob's actions towards him.

The challenging truth of the matter, however, is that this fight was instigated by those closest to them, the ones that they ideally should have been able to trust. The fight did not stop Esau from seeing multiplication, but it did change his path.

Hopefully, by now, we realize the fallacy of, "Sticks and stones may break my bones but words, will never hurt." The words that Esau heard went to the core of himself. Something was snatched from him because his brother Jacob tricked him out of his birthright, but the truth is, in time, Esau was healed.

When you have a war happening in your mind, it affects your body and soul. Some of us must fight labels, fight ideas, and the hardest one is the fight within yourself. You do not have to be defined by what you have experienced, the mistakes or choices that you made. Although our experiences can teach us a lot about our strengths and weaknesses, it does not sum up the totality of who we are. When we are thrown off course, it can be challenging to get back without the right tools, fuel, and motivation.

Being thrown off the norm can bring increased stress and anxious feelings because everything is unfamiliar. This is a fight!

The words spoken to you can help frame your ideas, concepts, and expectations or lack thereof. In the case of Jacob and Esau, it would determine their quality of life.

In many conversations, I have heard people discuss the trauma they've experienced at the hands of family. This is not to bash any of our family, but rather to raise awareness of where some of our deep-seated issues can originate. Although we love our families, this is one of the first places we must set healthy boundaries to cancel the fight, for the fight can continue if not challenged and overthrown. Jacob tricked Esau, but he was later tricked by his uncle, his mother's brother Laban. It is suggestive that this side of his family embraced this type of behavior. If we don't evaluate the damage that can be caused in the name of family, then the likelihood of sharing toxic behavior with future generations is great.

I've shared conversations about individuals struggling with their self-esteem because of unhealthy joking from family: name-calling, derogatory remarks that eat at their confidence.

I was on the beach one day with a young guy and he had on long pants. Upon inquiry, he shared that he didn't like the way his legs looked. As we discussed further, his family making fun of his legs was the root cause of his fight with his self-image.

Yet in another conversation, a person revealed the struggle with her weight was because it was always a negative conversation and comparison within family. In an intimate setting, one young lady shared how she was being abused by a family member, but this was the same one that would call her fat and ugly, which caused her to suffer with bulimia. Some are struggling with substance abuse because someone thought it was a good idea to share alcohol and drugs with a child, and a habit was created.

None of us are perfect nor could think that these behaviors are correct, but if we trace the origins and negative outcomes back to the source, we must be willing to adjust and dismiss behaviors when recognized.

Some words are spoken to break you down intentionally. Some dismissive behaviors are intentional to get you to second-guess yourself and shrink. Whether the fight originates from words or deed, it still causes you to be in fist-swinging mode.

Being in constant fist-swinging mode causes stress on our being.

There are some fights that bring anxious feelings and we must know how to come out of fight mode. When we remain in fight mode too long, we expend energy on fighting when we could be building something positive.

However, when things are thrown at you, you must choose to survive but the danger can present itself when you are out of the moment, and you remain in fighting position. You could unknowingly keep out things that are beneficial for you.

Adversity is sure to be present ... what will we do when it comes?

I've read the story and adversity of Daniel being in the lion's den and know that the result was that God delivered him. (Daniel 6:16 KJV) What do I do in my den, when I can feel the heat from life's pressures and fires, when I can feel the growl of the lion without any exit strategy in place? What do you do when there seems to be no numbers to dial, or even if there are, they are not able to assist, or will not? At this point, there must be a choice, a conscious decision, to sink or swim.

Well, Lord knows I had been in some sink-or-swim scenarios, and I chose to take a deep breath and swim. The choice to swim does not negate feeling the strong current or the tide being high. This was not a back float in calm waters of a resort pool, but huge waves crashing against me, with dark skies and lonely spaces. I had to choose to fight, but I had to release the fight of self so that I had strength to fight through this den, this ocean of challenges in my life.

In the summer of 2017, I experienced an anxiety attack for the first time ever in life. It was at a time that so many little things were happening, amounting to a great thing. There were changes that were bringing me great challenges, but I am sure someone would have loved to have been in my shoes.

I am fortunate to have had it when my husband was around, and he supported me through it, but it was one of the craziest feelings in the world. It is an experience that I do not want to have happen again. I began to shake uncontrollably, and my mind was racing as I was in the fetal position. I was able to make it through it, but I really didn't understand why I would experience anxiety at this time, because I had overcome many other challenges without ever having this feeling. WHAT was different? WHY the fight, why now?

I felt that I was quite resilient and could face the challenge and keep going. I had fought many obstacles and was standing strong. But this time it wasn't the same. I was fighting for normalcy, something that I could relate to. I didn't recall having any close friends in my life that shared an experience like this before, so I didn't feel that I had many that could relate.

Once I experienced this, I knew that I had to do something different. My thoughts were foggy and it was difficult to concentrate on things. This increased my fight because I was trying to make sense of what was happening. I knew that I carried many responsibilities, and several people depended on me, but I didn't want to let anyone down, including myself. If you have ever experienced a scenario like this, that has you all out of sorts, you must be much more intentional about self-care. I knew that I couldn't be a rescue boat to everyone else with a hole in mine.

I knew that I had to process and trace the entry point of this feeling of anxiety. I didn't like it and I know it was some of my current circumstances that were fueling it. I had to take time to process all the spaces that seemed frazzled.

Your enemy would love for you to give up and fight in silence. Your adversary would hope to burden you down so much that you don't want to fight. The fact that I did not allow myself to suffer in silence or allow shame to grip me empowered me. I was able to be honest about the moment and strip the demon of secrecy of any power over me. The enemy was stripped of his power to cause shame because I found safety in wise counsel. God directed me to two specific people, other than my husband, to share this incident with. The beautiful thing is that they were prepared for my call, had already been praying for me. They were a safe place for me to dump this and fostered a dialogue that could help to identify and uproot the culprit.

It was not until I shared this experience that I realized so many others had dealt with it before and overcame. What if I had just sat in silence? That spirit of anxiety would have been in violation and hoping for a seat to stay, aiming to steal my peace and joy.

I knew some of what I was fighting was about who I am and being convinced that I couldn't do what God has chosen me to do. I did choose to speak to a therapist to process things, as well as my physician, but because I had some insight on some of the origin, I did not want to mask anything with medication. I wanted to confront and heal. It was vitally important for me to process *all* the stuff that was happening. I had to change up my strategy and do something different, not just what I was accustomed to, because I was experiencing another level of intensity and knew that some of it was a spiritual fight.

I had to be intentional about relaxation and guard my thoughts even more. I had to increase the health of my thoughts because I was still dealing with external factors that could apply pressure. This is why moving on autopilot cannot be our means to function. When our scenarios change, we must make proper adjustments and break our norms.

My thoughts could release or apply pressure: I chose to be on the side that would release pressure. I had to be strategic about what I would speak, regardless of the circumstances I was facing, and there were many present. I used my words to frame my world and my mind.

> *"I had fainted, unless I had believed to see the goodness of the Lord in the land of the living. Wait on the lord: be on good courage, and he shall strengthen thine heart: wait I say, on the Lord."*
> (Psalms 27:13,14, KJV)

Although there was nothing that I liked about having an anxiety attack, it pushed me to an assessment; it made me do what I knew how to do ... excavate and evaluate. I had to confront where I was. It was a fragile time that ultimately became a strengthening time for me.

I had to speak to my body, to my spirit and, more importantly, guard my ears. I realized that this space in my life could not be shared with everyone; it wouldn't be understood. I didn't want to invite an unnecessary struggle trying to explain this process to anyone, other than whom God told me to share it with. My effort had to be ongoing so that I could come through this on top. I was more strategic about my day and what I consumed.

I realized that my current space, the *den*, the fighting ring, had so much that I did not recognize. The lack of normalcy was perpetuating the fight. I didn't have my career, co-workers, work friends, not even my normal church family. We had recently experienced a major transition in our family that left us vulnerable. I realized that I could not hold on to a space that God had moved me from. I had to do what I was born to do—create. I had to create comforts where I was. I had to stay fresh and I knew much of what I was experiencing was a part of me being stretched. My present circumstances were also bringing challenges for me to do things that I did not feel equipped to do. I quickly learned some of my hidden talents in this space but didn't feel qualified to do what I had to. I had a standard for myself and I was experiencing revisions.

In one of the most pressurized times, I was able to embrace and articulate my strengths because I had to focus on what was good, what was right and what I was good at, and not how I was feeling. If I had rested on my emotions alone, the anxiety may have increased. I poured out in a safe place, put tools in place to fortify my thoughts, and I accepted a new space. Right in the middle of a fight I had to embrace something new. Could it be that what I was holding in my mind instigated the fight? I believe so! Think about things, whether good or bad, that you have been holding on to. Some things can't travel to your new space. You fight with what was and what is present and to come, and this creates a lot of pressure.

You must be willing to let go of everything that caused you to fight with yourself up until this point. You need to release it for you and your family. There must be revisions and they can start with you.

When you are presented with a fight …
swing, create, but don't stay on the ropes;
make the necessary changes

The acceptance of a new space shifted my expectation and focus. I begin to focus more on now; I appreciated more of today. I gained new skills because I was intentional with pouring into myself. I gained a new level of trust in God and myself. This fight changed me. When you fight, you spend energy going over what has occurred but when you fight to be free, you filter that energy into creating an exit plan so that you win. When you are presented with a fight … swing, create, but don't stay on the ropes; make the necessary changes.

> *"You will have to fight to live, and you will be a slave to your brother. But when you fight to be free, you will break away from his control."*
> (Genesis 27:40, ERV)

Anything that has tried to expel your energy, you have the authority to break away from it.

Chapter 13

THE IT OF VIOLATION

The spirit of violation can create widespread pandemonium in our culture and if we just continue to skip over this area, we do not halt the issues that come along with it. Trauma can enter when we experience violation, as it is a forceful entry that can break us down. When anyone or anything is violated, taken advantage of, forcefully hurt, sexually and verbally misused, it wrenches the heart of the person. The spirit of violation is a thief that has been able to intertwine in our community as "normal."

> **The spirit of violation is a thief that has been able to intertwine in our community as "normal."**

This thief has been able to hide in plain sight in our homes, workplaces, and communities, but is one of the greatest enemies of our time. Violation affects the mind, body, and spirit.

I have shared conversations with many that have experienced violation, whether it be sexual, emotional, or verbal, and the common denominator is pain—a heart-wrenching pain. This IT can and will cause identity crises if not confronted.

The story of Amnon and Tamar in the holy Bible, 2 Samuel 2:13, comes to mind as I think of sexual violation. Amnon had a desire for his sister Tamar and used trickery and manipulation to get to her. She was in what was supposed to be a safe environment. She went to tend to her "sick" brother at King David's command, but Amnon had a trickster in his ear that told him a plan to take advantage of a girl trying to help him—his sister. He literally had no regard for her heart or her actions, as his mind was one-dimensional. He wanted her and when she refused, he did it anyway. She asked him not to violate her and posed the question, "How do I get rid of my disgrace and shame?" The rape was one aspect, but the treatment thereafter was worse for her. He violated her virginity, so now she would have to bear the public notice of that: previously she dressed according to her virginal status, but now she had to dress for her violated status. He stripped higher status from her, he was rude to her after the attack as if she had done something wrong, and commanded that she be thrown out and the doors bolted behind her. She went in hiding with shame and disgrace, but *she* was the victim. She took pride in being able to wear her gown of colors, but she subsequently marked her head with dust as a sign of grief. This spirit of violation made her lose status, identity, and control over that area of her life.

Her brother Absalom knew about her violation and told her to keep silent about it. She went into seclusion. King David was notified of the offense, but he was in a precarious situation because this had to do with family. He did not act, and this caused discord among his relatives.

What a situation to be in, but it happens too often.

Many are violated in the place where they should feel safe and have refuge, and too many turn their heads as if it never happened. Some have even been told that it happens to everyone. Yet, when we see the behaviors that can stem from this entry point, it's not always realized how they started. Because of the ignorance of the origin, we treat symptoms and not the wound—the root is still left untouched.

There is no doubt Tamar was dealing with grief and anger. She lost a part of her, but she kept living, kept moving. Some things had changed but life had to go on. Life must go on, but you can't just skip over the offense like it never happened. This family felt the effects of this act. There was contention amongst the house of David. Absalom had a difficult time dealing with this offense and it took him out of character. The situation wasn't dealt with and he did not forget, so he made it his mission to do something about it. What if the family came together and hashed this thing out, gave it some room to air out, breathe and heal, as opposed to acting like it never occurred? Maybe all parties would have been able to come to a resolution.

Instead, Absalom made this act part of the fabric of his life. Maybe he could have been putting energy into the greatness of his purpose and destiny, but his sister's rape and hurt was stealing from him. The violation was no longer just about her, and it never is. This IT threw Tamar and Absalom into an identity crisis, where she went into seclusion and he sought revenge. He literally allowed this offense to consume him. He plotted revenge; he became disrespectful to his father and others; he morphed into a different person. He felt that he had to do something to avenge his sister.

I imagine he asked questions like, "What do I do now? How do I function after this?" Did Absalom wait to hear the answers, or did he keep it moving?

Unresolved and deep-rooted pain must be dealt with and ejected from your life. There are times that you may never get to face your violator, but you must face the violation. The ability to face the act will bind and destroy the thief in your life: the thief of joy, creativity, love, and intimacy.

One of the major emotions that can stem from violation of any kind is anger—but especially sexual violation. There are some people that you may have seen change in their lives and emotions after experiencing violation. If the anger is not handled, it can certainly progress to a rebellion, because an "I don't care attitude" can form. Violation can be more difficult when the victim knows their violator and he/she acts if they had a right to violate. It can be even more intense when the violator openly disrespects the victim. This type of offense always affects in layers.

Any male or female that has been subjected to sexual violation can relate. I had a personal experience as a young adult that left me walking away feeling confused. "Was I just raped?" I wondered. I know that this may seem weird to some, but there are scenarios that can present blurred lines. I liked the guy; I wasn't forced to be at his home or in his presence, but I was not ready to sleep with him. I was interested in spending time with him, but I realized that our ideas were different. Well, IT happened and his treatment of me immediately changed. I'm certain that he could feel the resistance, but I was already there. This was a time where previous violations made me feel powerless. His treatment of me was like Amnon's of Tamar. I had horrible feelings, a thousand questions, and he drove me home at 90 miles an hour (literally) and never spoke to me in the same manner again. All chivalry was out the door, contact was lost, and yucky feelings were present.

At the time, I only shared these feelings with my best friend. I cried almost all day and I certainly didn't know what to do. I was clear of the scrutiny that comes along with saying you have been violated. The pain from that will make you feel like you should just keep silent. It was two decades later before I saw him again.

It was a beautiful Sunday morning and my husband was scheduled to minister at a prominent church in my hometown. There he was, a deacon in the front row. I am not sure if he ever saw me or would know who I was if he did. The memories flooded. I don't know if I realized that they were undealt with, but the bad things were the main memories I had about him. It was a challenging worship service for me, because here I was with my family, processing in silence. It was at that moment I decided to release any pain associated with this scenario.

This is a prime example of forgiving someone that may not realize you are holding on to something. I didn't realize it. This is the importance of processing matters and not shelving them. He may have never viewed this scenario as "wrong," but I know it wasn't right for me. Of course, I went through the process of questioning in my mind, "Did I send the wrong message to him? Was I being too sensitive?" I never had a chance to confront him with any of this. The best option for me was to release. I did, and I shared it with my husband AFTER that service, which proved to be an even greater part of my healing.

I, like many others, have experienced sexual violation more than once. It does something to your psyche. It causes a need to hide within yourself; if you are not able to get help, you shrink in plain sight.

The spirit of violation can cause you to say an unwilling yes. Once someone or something has violated your person, you may struggle with saying no. But you must realize that you have a right to say no, and you must learn how to set healthy boundaries.

One of the most natural responses to violation is to keep everyone out but it is not our best option. We must take the time to learn how to use a gate, to control entry and exit in our lives, but the wall keeps everything and everyone out. It creates restrictions that can continually violate you and allow constant victimization. If you don't attain healing, walls will remain. Walls create hardship, are difficult to see beyond, and require a great amount of energy to scale. If you were violated, you'll want to reach the point of freedom where you can demolish the wall.

You must heal that headspace, so you don't find yourself dumbing down, or in situations that you leave feeling violated again.

There are various ways that you must free yourself. Counseling is a great outlet; couple it with prayer and write a letter to the violator. It's not for you to write with the intention to put it in his/her hand or face, but for you to be able to say all the things that you would want to say and clear the hard drive of your heart and mind, so you can eject the thief. The thief comes but to steal, kill, and destroy: you are worth too much to allow anyone or anything to violate you again and steal from you. Make a choice to face your violation.

Make a choice to prevent violation from stealing from you any-more. When the violator has left but is still holding you hostage, he/she gets to operate in a space in your life that is undeserved.

If you allow the memory of violation to haunt you, it has the poten-tial to make you morph into something out of character and you'll stay off course. However, if you process the pain and overcome it, use it as a point of reference for the victory in your life, as opposed to a tool of bondage, then you will experience release and freedom. There is a gentleness that God gave to all of us because of His fruit of the spirit. We must not allow our hearts to be clouded by offense. We must remember that Satan's goal is to kill, steal, and destroy, and that includes our authentic personali-ties and characteristics. Incidents in our lives that are not ejected will aim to take a seat and bring a contrary design to replace God's original one. Galatians 5: 22,23 (KJV) says, "But the fruit of the spirit is love, joy, peace, longsuffering, gentleness, goodness, faith, meekness, temperance, against such there is no law." The negative things that happen in our lives can always bring a great outcome, even if it does not feel like it when it happens. I wish violation on no one but the point to drive here is that you don't have to allow the perpetrator to steal from you. Process the event, get therapy, counseling, coaching-whatever works for you, but eject the viola-tion. It has taken from you long enough.

If you allow the memory of violation to haunt you, it has the potential to make you morph into something out of character and you'll stay off course.

Genesis 50:20 KJV: *"But as for you, ye thought evil against me, but God meant it unto good, to bring to pass, as it is this day, to save much people alive."*

You survived it, which means you have the power to overcome it.

1. Have you ever been violated?
2. Have you shared your pain in a safe place?
3. Do you have memories that make you feel low?
4. Have you sought therapy?

Chapter 14

WHEN IT CAUSES YOU TO FEAR

G od has not given us the spirit of fear, but of power, of love, and a sound mind (2 Timothy 1:7, KJV). Fear works to remove the soundness of your mind and decisions. There is a certain resistance to something you have never attempted before, or something noted as unsafe. This piece of insight will cause you to think about what you are going to attempt; this would be a healthy fear or evaluation. Then there is the debilitating, leg-shaking, confidence-snatching, second-guessing spirit of FEAR, not welcome in any of our lives.

Fear can change your life and will if it is not ejected.

Fear can change your life and will if it is not ejected.

Have you ever second-guessed yourself? The answer is highly likely yes, but we are not supposed to live there. We are not supposed to live in a constant place of uncertainty, and this type of behavior can cause stress and toxic behavior. The presence of fear will have us missing opportunities through being consumed by all the things that might happen and have never happened.

Fear comes in all shapes and forms: fear of failure, fear of repeating a cycle, fear that you can't do it or won't do it. The Bible declares that "God has not given us the spirit of fear, but of power, love and sound mind" (2 Tim. 1:7, KJV).

If God, our creator, has not given this to us, then where did it come from?

We learn it; we see those around us operate in it; we hear it in our environments and many times it is subtle. God is gracious to give us instruction for this journey called life, but it does not always present with certainties. Sometimes we don't know the outcome of our scenarios, so we must have and develop our faith. Faith gives us the willingness to depend on God, regardless of our scenarios, and our love for Him encourages us to lean back and trust Him. So, although we may not know what's next, we know that God has our best interests at heart for this life that He has given to us.

If you entertain the IT of fear instead of casting it down, it will try to rule your life. Things that you never second-guessed now come into question. The conspiracies can form in your head and mind, and the goal is to strip you of your peace and power, period. The enemy does not play fair. Some of us experienced entry points of fear from family, the schoolyard, etc. Sometimes it was through "harmless games" and "friendly taunts."

If the games and fun caused a seed of fear to root, then they are not harmless and friendly.

A common example of this is some adults are afraid of dogs because someone thought it was funny to allow an infant to be chased by a strange, little, barking thing. The adult recognized and understood it to be a dog, but the child saw it as something foreign and threatening. Others may be dealing with a fear of the dark because a family member thought it was a good idea to lock you in the closet for punishment or fun and ignore your cry for help, only being told to be quiet. What about losing control in a swimming pool or tub of water and not going back to the water again? Several situations introduce entry points and the factor of the unknown into people's lives. Being without the ability to trust can create fear. These include a failed relationship, the fear of abandonment, being alone, rejection, and violation. Sometimes when we face these issues, we never look at these incidents for what they are, missing the opportunity to process the pain. When things happen in our lives that are beyond our control, we must be able to come to a resolution in that area; we must go back to face the entry point as soon as possible.

I can recall an incident in our lives with one of our small children.

One day, I was coming into my garage and our son was just a toddler, maybe fourteen months old. As we were getting out of the car, his dad came to greet us and went back in the house. The baby and I were still in the garage with the door raised. I looked up and a beautiful, gray pit bull came into my garage. The baby's back was turned, and the dog ran between us. I watched this dog tower over my baby, its face close to his. I was uncertain about the dog's intentions. I wasn't sure if she was going to attack and I felt helpless.

I did not want to make a sudden move because this was not my dog and I'd never had any interaction with her prior to now. My adrenaline began to flow to the point where my knees were shaking because I could see this dog towering over my kid—I screamed to my husband and the tone of my voice sent him into HIGH alert. Before he could make it back to the garage, our son turned, pointed his finger, and firmly told the dog "NO." By that time, my husband stood in the middle of the garage, picked our son up, put him on top of the car, and I went on top too. I later realized that the dog was a puppy and wanted to play. Now that the kid was out of her reach, she ran into our house. Knowing that we were secure, my hubby got the dog out and took her back to her owner. The unfamiliarity of that scenario had my heart racing and I'm certain our son's heart was racing too. The dog's stature was a bit intimidating. I was feeling nervous, but I wanted to be sure that there was no entry point that would make him not want to be around dogs. I was really happy about the confidence displayed by our son, but I know that it was a little knee-shaking. I gave it a little time and I called a different neighbor, explained the situation, and asked if I could come to her house and see her dog. We knew this dog and it was a smaller puppy. I wanted to see how my son functioned around the dog and reintroduce him to a dog in a calm environment. I didn't want a fear of dogs to enter him and take root. I teach my children that we don't bother dogs if we don't know them or if it's not okay with their owner. I teach them boundaries with unfamiliar animals. I DID NOT want an incident to cause fear of an entire species of animals for our children. Dogs are a regular part of life, so I wanted him to be able to function well.

My neighbor agreed. When my son and I walked into their house, we moved slowly and initially he was hesitant, resistant. I was a bit emotional when I saw his resistance and that fear had creeped in. I felt the knee shaking feeling although we were in a different environment with a different dog. We faced the resistance and stayed at the neighbor's home. I wanted the reminder of loving dogs to surface opposed to the knee shaking reminder of the unfamiliar pit bull. We did it a few times and he was able to be around dogs and enjoy playing with them. Although the incident with the pit bull occurred, it wasn't able to steal from him. I recently spoke to an adult male that still has a fear of dogs because he had a bad experience as a child that he has never confronted. No one challenged that incident for him, so the entire species of dogs cannot be enjoyed by him, because of a moment.

Our daughter has a natural love for water. She was about eighteen months old the first time she went in a pool, but she went in confidently. We were moving between the pool and jacuzzi and she wanted to take off her floaties while in the jacuzzi. I allowed her to do so and she was doing great. At one point, while underwater, she reached for the bar in the jacuzzi and it slipped from her hand. I was standing over her and when she lost control, I saw the fear in her face. I stepped into the water and brought her up. I didn't react, just made her cough to ensure her lungs were clear, and that she was okay. She was calm. I gave her some instructions, gave her a few moments, put her floaties back on, and got in the water with her. She was showing some resistance, but I knew she loved water and I did not want fear from her little mishap to grip her. I wanted to halt the possibility of fear of the water, so we coached her gently back into the water and to this day, she still enjoys water as opposed to allowing it to steal from her. We gave instructions, boundaries, and guidelines until she mastered swimming and gained personal confidence in her skills.

Fear's goal is to stop you, but the good news is it doesn't own you nor do you take instructions from IT. There are entry points of fear that you must trace back, confront, and uproot. Fear desires to hide in your life as something else so that you don't give it the boot. It requires you to evaluate and put some thought into areas of your life.

Are you operating beneath your ability? If so, WHY? Did something stop you in your tracks?

Fear will cause one's mind to go out of sync with the truth and much of what you should be enjoying you will not be able to engage in because of fear. It is necessary to go back to some of those moments that stuff looked you in the face, and look back at it. Confront the dark closets that tried to grip you and steal your mobility.

1. Can you recall a frightening moment in your life?
2. Did you allow this moment to shape your future?
3. Can you think of some areas that you need to confront that will cast down fear?

Chapter 15

WHEN IT CAUSES YOU TO LOSE CONFIDENCE

There are events in our lives that can shake us to the point that we shrink. When we realize that timidity is not an authentic place in the fabric of life, it must be identified and ejected; this point is non-negotiable. If one is knocked down and doesn't strive to get up, the posture changes. The longer you stay down, the chances are greater that you'll experience loss in your physical and mental muscle and tenacity. The pebbles (IT) that cause you to lose confidence in yourself can lead to confinement, because of the boundaries and limitations that you place on yourself. What was once attainable is now viewed as an obstacle that cannot be overcome. The difference between overcoming, standing up, and staying down is the thought process to see yourself victoriously and seeing yourself in a winning posture, the ability to encourage yourself and your vision beyond the present. We must see ourselves beyond the point of interruption.

I experienced a situation in my work that altered my life. It affected some of my physical capacity, which ultimately affected my home life. My sleep pattern was off, my exercise regimen was off, and my energy level was altered. I found myself feeling frustrated and challenged with who I was because there was so much that I did not recognize, especially physically. Without the outside world knowing some of the challenges, I had to deal with the scrutiny of change. Others were viewing me in a way that they had never seen me before. However, I had to realize that I didn't owe an explanation to them, especially if there was no constructive conversation with them. The fact that I guarded that area did not remove the inner battle happening inside.

I experienced rapid weight gain due to some synthetic drugs I was on, which seemed like one of the hardest problems to face because I was accustomed to being within a certain weight range. If I had sat on the couch and ate Twinkies and gallons of ice cream all day, maybe it would not have been as difficult to face. But I trusted the advice of the physicians caring for me and this was where I landed. I experienced many emotions, anger being one of them, because I felt like I was left hanging and I was still experiencing pain.

So here I was, thirty pounds heavier, sleep pattern off, and the eyes of people to face. I quickly realized how harsh words could be. Let me just insert this here, if a person has experienced weight gain, he/she is the first to notice, so your insult is unnecessary. I was able to separate the pebble-throwers from those who were genuinely concerned. Some would say changes are normal and should be expected to some degree, but I believe that the pain and the change are what affected me. I had to learn how to respond in a healthy manner to the probing or negativity because all conversations could not be avoided.

I don't believe that a person should lose sight of self because of a weight shift, but it can indeed create emotional and physical weights—for me it did. I have heard people respond to a 20-pound weight gain not because the person is obese but because of abnormality, and a person's reality should never be minimized because it is not the same as yours. But the challenge was getting beyond that point of abrupt change and beyond speculation or wondering if I could lose the weight. Would this be my new normal? I struggled with moving my single-digit clothes out of the closet, trading them for some sizes that were double digits. I began to struggle in my own skin and at someone else's hand. I really had to have a "come to Jesus" moment and know that this did not change who I was—it changed some physical things, but not my core. Working in the healthcare industry allowed me to see others that experienced life-altering events and hear stories of people whose injuries prevented them from exercising. So, I began a thank-you party. "Thank you, Lord, that I am able to move this body part." "Thank you, Lord, that I have this body part." "Thank you, Lord, that I am motivated to do something." I had to shift my perspective to meet this challenge, but it weighed on my mind more than I thought. I second-guessed many things I never had before, all because of an interruption. I had to assess my life. Nowhere in the manual (what manual?) does it say that there will not be interruptions or challenges in life, for they are inevitable.

I had to experience acceptance. I had to accept that this pebble was here, but I used my mouth to express my gratitude. I was grateful that I could do something about it. I had to be grateful that I was able to feel. I went on a shopping spree and purchased things that would let me feel comfortable and good about myself and where I was. I had to refuse to compare myself to my previous self and embrace me in the present. I also had to release some of the negative and undermining comments in and out of work. What was an annoyance to some had literally shifted my life and how I functioned. Some of the basic activities that I did before without thinking now had a level of physical pain associated with them. My confidence was in question and my courage to try certain things was low.

We don't know every day of our lives, but God does; so we must seek His will and way and thoughts for guidance. We must be willing to embrace the place, challenge, or incident that occurred and know that we are resilient to endure and overcome. I don't have a right to be timid; it's not who I am—but if I don't eject it, then it becomes comfortable and the confidence becomes shaky. Sometimes what we view as an interruption is a change in path that is purposed and beneficial; because it's unfamiliar, we cannot always see the benefit of it. That is why we must hold on and endure the process of change, because if we do, we get to see the benefits.

I once heard a story of a woman that decided to leave her prestigious job; one that she loved and paid her well. She had a place of security and comfort and an opportunity to take a risk. She was at a crossroads. This would be a prime example of why we would want to eject things that discourage you and fight your confidence, because when you are faced with hard decisions, you want to be able to move and think clearly.

The ability to make choices and think critically can be stagnated by a lack of confidence, but staying in one position will never afford us the opportunity to know our greater selves.

This woman pushed on with a promise from God, but also with uncertainty in her mind. She now owns several successful franchise restaurants that yield her income many times over what she was receiving in her former workplace of comfort and security. We are not always sure what God wants to give to us, but we must eject lack of confidence because it will distort our vision to consider moving forward. Lack of confidence has the potential to lock your knees and tie your hands, so you must confront it so that it does not steal your forward progression.

We cannot allow murder attempts (the things that wanted to kill your spirit) on us to succeed. The entry point of an IT shouldn't be allowed to take your ability to make progress, so whatever incident occurred in your life that wants you to cower, shrinking in purpose and personality, today I want you to confront it.

Identify what it is, embrace the fact that some things have changed; now make steps to move in the right direction and do so in power and purpose. On the other side of this "interruption" are things greater than what you have seen, but you must grasp that concept first to attain it. If you lose confidence in yourself, then you invite stagnation and frustration. The thing that once fought my confidence was the very thing that made me seriously consider choosing another career. Just like the lady's story above, I know that risking my comfort and taking the leap will be beneficial and reward me and my family.

The vision of your true self, purpose, and identity is always bigger than you, more than how your view yourself. The drama, the work, the finances that it takes to achieve will always require you to stretch beyond your present state. So if you are confident of who you are and know your purpose ... stretch further, for there is more. If you don't have purpose identified and know what makes you thrive, think and stretch beyond where you are. What we all have in common is ... there is more, there is greater, and we need God to accomplish it all.

> **The vision of your true self, purpose, and iden-tity is always bigger than you, more than how your view yourself**

Seeing your vision, accepting your authenticity is your responsibility; provision is God's responsibility. Your perspective and perception will change once you hear, embrace, and see your purpose. What once seemed foreign will be tangible and you will be challenged to GO LARGER because we are in constant evolution. You will always have to do something greater than what you have before.

> *"So don't lose the courage that you had in the past. Your courage will be rewarded richly. You must be patient. After you have done what God wants, you will get what he promised you."* (Hebrews 10:34-35, ERV)

1. Has there been changes in your life that caused you to lose confidence?
2. How did you confront those changes?
3. Did you experience growth from the changes?

Chapter 16

THE IT OF GRIEF

When we experience losses, take hits, and get the wind knocked out of us, we experience grief. It may be an obvious entry of grief when one experiences loss of a loved one. But what about other areas that cause us grief and we don't realize it? What happens when we don't realize what a scenario has taken from us? There are mental challenges associated with loss, hardship, and pain.

When we experience losses, take hits, and get the wind knocked out of us, we experience grief.

Have you ever experienced any hardship in your life? Most of us have, but how we view it at the point and beyond the point of pain can have a lasting effect on our lives.

The loss of anything can cause grief: of a loved one, job, career, home, finances, business deal, school offer, scholarship, relationship, physical ability or capacity, etc.

What do you do when loss happens? Do you act as though it never occurred? From my observations, the latter has never given a healthy or prosperous outcome to a person.

When a major shift or loss occurs, there has to be a regrouping and an effort to put a strategic plan in place. To move beyond the point, it is very important to see if there is anything to be gleaned from the experience. Was there anything you could have done to avoid the loss? For instance, when it comes to loss of a job, could there have been a better effort made on your part? Were there any aspects you could have improved? On the other hand, it could be that none of the aforementioned factors played a role in the loss. It could have been the luck of the draw: company downsizing, seniority, the phasing out of a position—but we should always want to make personal evaluation of our efforts. This allows us to assume responsibility and be accountable for our part in a scenario. These are evaluations that can help us to grow and not repeat some negative actions.

We can also experience loss that we don't have control of, e.g., life and death and the cycle of it or the events surrounding it. However, whether in control or not, we must confront loss of any kind.

To ignore that these types of things have happened to us can permit a level of unhealthy stress on our lives. We want to avoid unhealthy stress and process grief and its effects.

I was noting a conversation from one of the parents of a 9/11 victim. She stated that it took her years to grieve. I believe this happens more than we realize, and we operate in a fragmented state, experiencing a constant moving of the mind and not resting properly until we complete the process of healing or, for some, simply addressing the loss and beginning to heal. The avoidance behavior can take a toll on us physically and emotionally.

As I was wrapping up writing this book, I had an epiphany. In previous chapters, I wrote about the challenge with becoming mute, the feeling of being on an island, the attack of anxiety, and my search for normalcy after a major move. I began to think about all the major changes that happened over the course of five years, good and bad, and I had THE moment. I was aware of losses and apparent grief, but I never grieved the loss of my career.

The lack of resolve in that area of walking away from my career compounded the losses that I had experienced in this new geographical location.

Although initially it was not my intention to leave my career when I moved up north, it was what I realized was happening. When I tracked the fact that I had made several out-of-state moves and had not experienced some of what I had with this move, I found the source. This was a major rock thrown in my pond and it literally shifted my life. I have worked since the age of sixteen, starting a business as a teenager. I did hair for friends and family prior to becoming a board-certified cosmetologist. I used this same work as a stylist to help in my pursuit of my healthcare career. Not only did I work, but I also managed the salon. Once I finished my studies and began work as an ultrasound technologist, I had to put my hairstyling skills to the side only because I relocated out of state and took a job in my new career. However, eventually I was comfortable in my environment and I serviced clients on weekends and evenings. I quickly got involved in my church and community events, music, mentoring, and extracurricular activities. I was able to thrive in new environments. Prior to being married with children, I had already lived in four states, so I was not afraid to move, start over, or try something new. Once we got married, we relocated as a couple to Virginia and again in 2013, New York became home. So I had to poke around and get to what was so different or challenging about this particular relocation. What was so different?

But this impactful move to the north was a move more centered around my husband. He was the one that was familiar with the environment, unlike me and the children. I was still excited about the move because the company I was working for had a location about 25 minutes from my house. So, I thought it was going to be a viable option to keep my time in the company and apply for a position in my new location. Much to my surprise, no jobs were listed in my field for months. This almost never happens; I should have at least been able to take a per-diem position. Because of the way the company's department was structured, it wouldn't let me see a post in my specialty because they combined their departments. In other facilities, my specialty was a separate entity. To complicate this idea, my hubby's schedule would not permit me to take a position that would require me to carry a pager to be on call, as I had most of my career working in a hospital. Nor did we have a support system in place that could help if I was called in to work for an emergency. This was a realistic expectation and just part of the territory. I would have needed to be available twenty-four hours some days.

I was also at a crossroads of sitting for a certification exam I knew I was not in the proper headspace to attempt. All these variables and a word from God let me settle on the fact that I was walking away from my career. Not sitting for this exam was closing it, logically, for good. I had to accept this idea and reach a peace about it. This wasn't the hard part, because I was clear that I did not want to retire as a sonographer when I started my career. This exit just wasn't looking like I thought it would. The challenge was once I closed the door, I kept moving and didn't grieve the loss. I didn't recognize the effect that it had on me.

I left not just a job of five years, but a career of thirteen years, and became a housewife: one with no friends, eight weeks postpartum, and no connections in church or community. This was a vulnerable space on so many levels. I would never have thought that my job defined me, but I realized I was missing a piece of me—I was missing work. I was really missing my interaction with people and patients, and my love of helping.

I never despised being a housewife, but I didn't put a lot of thought into it either. It was not something that I aimed for because I was accustomed to working away from the home. I can guarantee that if I was involved socially in my new move to New York as I had been in times past, or well-connected at church, this career change may not have bothered me at all, or at least not as much.

There would have been some involvement and I may not have felt like I was on the sidelines. I would have been contributing. I am an exhorter of potential and had been working with people for over twenty years, so to be pulled from that on every level, I later realized, presented hidden challenges. The great effect had to be the closing of the door on my career, because I had resigned from jobs and experienced unemployment before, but I had the option of working in the field again. I had moved before. I had started new positions and even worked in cities where I knew no one and lived alone there for months. These experiences were great. There were times in my life where I could have chosen several other options, but not this time. I had never relocated without a job opportunity. I didn't have any hair clients, no one knew me, and I certainly didn't just want strangers in my home—this was a new normal; not to mention being eight weeks post-partum.

I wanted to make this transition great for my family and me, but I know I felt vulnerable on so many levels and my husband knew it too. I was looking for my place in this transition.

It was a great opportunity for Jesse, and he had several on the table prior to this move, but we knew this was it...New York. We moved into a big house, on acres of land, and had a wonderful family to nurture, but I quickly realized the personal production and achievement portion was missing from my life. I was not involved on a business level in this location, nor was I personally connected.

I was grateful for the opportunity to recuperate and think that is what held off some of my desire to achieve personally outside my home for just a little while. I never realized how much work went into staying at home with little children full time.

Just before our baby turned a year old, after ten months of being in a new city, we decided to send the children to daycare. This would be great for their social skills and give their dad and I an opportunity to plant and build. I was fully engaged in nurturing my home, but I wasn't doing my best with self-care. I started a work-from-home job to do something that I enjoyed; this was more enjoyment than income-based. At this point, I could enjoy the work and build a business. But there were still no coffee dates with a friend, or a girls' meeting at the house or a work meeting to go to, and it was like this for years. The crazy thing is I enjoyed being available and being at home, but I wanted to see some things thrive personally.

During this transition of the move, I got in the habit of being up all night and not sleeping until morning. This was partly due to being a nursing mom but it was not a healthy pattern; it was exhausting. I left a place where I could stand in the yard and talk to several neighbors, laughing, crying and dancing, to come to a neighborhood where I may not see a neighbor for days. I had co-workers that I could enjoy while working and some had become like family.

Grief had woven itself into the fabric of my everyday life and I simply kept pushing through it all. Fast-forward years later when some real-life challenges came, I was already compromised in my emotions. That is why there was a fragility. I was able to be rattled easier, experiencing irritability and emotional weakness.

We gave up everything for my husband to take this position, which was seemingly terminated without much thought. We became as sitting ducks in an open pond. That scenario brought emotions that had to be processed appropriately. But to complicate it, we couldn't depend on me or my former career to sustain us or hold it—I had walked away. Can you imagine the emotions that hit both of us? The thing that I hadn't grieved and didn't have today as an option, (returning to my job) could possibly have been the thing that helped us out of this tight spot. I could have lightened this load a little. These were thoughts that crowded my mind, along with all the readjusting we now had to do with my hubby's loss of contract —new grief. His job shifted, and I didn't have a career to support us.

I realize that this was why some of the other things were so big for me. I was facing hardship and had to process all the layers. I knew that there was a reason I had to walk away; I was glad I'd walked away, but I also had to reinvent myself.

What would you do now? You and your family have now experienced job loss, loss of home, and death of relatives over a short timeframe. How will you make it? Why won't you move? Why won't you relocate? I was thinking, "God, if we are going to struggle, we can go home and at least be with our family and friends that really care about us." What shall we do?

In the middle of all these changes and questions, we got a call from a friend and ministry colleague. It had been a while since we had spoken to her so when I saw her number on the phone, I knew it was important. She asked us to come to church that night because she was in town, but it was almost time for service to start and we were away from home. However, she was persistent, insisting, "You have time." We didn't know why but we felt compelled to go.

We arrived at service at 10:00pm; that could have been our first deterrent, but we somehow knew we needed to be there. I had to step out briefly to assist one of the children, but Jesse went up and sang with our friend. As they were ministering, she turned to him and said, "Jesse, I don't know what you have been going through, but the Lord says "DON'T MOVE! Something great is coming down the pipeline!" We had to be assured that God was giving us the answer, to stay put and tough out the storm. This was an encouragement as we were processing the losses.

This charge pushed us even harder to reinvent ourselves. I was already working on things to transform myself, but I was even more determined now. Although I knew I had to stay here in New

York, there was great adversity looking us in the face. My faith pushed me to say, "If God said stay, I trust HIM!"

I started taking more classes to shift myself into a new career. I had to pull out my strengths and skillset attached to my previous career that were transferrable, as well as others I had gained, but none of this was yielding me much income. I was working from the heart but without pay. ALL I COULD DO WAS TRUST AND KEEP WORKING.

I knew that one of my major focuses with this New York move was to keep my family in balance, something that helped me through the process. That is all that some of the people in my new area knew of me. They knew me as a mom and Jesse's wife. I didn't really have a personal identity. I was present in many places, but I realized how superficial my relationships were in this new place. I am fortunate to have made family balance a priority in my career. If I had not, this stay-at-home-mom job, it may have caused me to crash. If work was the main thing to me, I may have lost it. I have always expressed the importance of a healthy work-life balance in my career. I was now having to fully implement this. I had to keep my priorities in check and remember the Lord made it clear that we were to make this move up north. The obedience of writing this book brought an entirely new level of acceptance and healing, helping me find the culprit of what I had been fighting with.

In July 2016, I received a gut-wrenching call that one of my sisters, and best friends, had suddenly died. It was a major blow, which exacerbated the lack of conflict resolution in other areas of my life: the career loss, the "island" experience and the lack of personal production.

The call caused me to scream so loud that my husband, who was out in the garden, came running in. Nothing could have made me believe that I would be experiencing this—not her, not now.

I prayed; I asked God for a miracle; I asked Him to breathe life back into her and I was waiting. I was waiting to hear of her movement in the morgue. I asked again, "Lord, if it's in Your will, please perform this miracle. Astound the physicians; work a present-day miracle, PLEASE."

However, I had to come to terms and embrace the reality of this loss.

We spent the first few weeks getting past the services and celebrations of life, but when all that was over, reality set in. My sister, my buddy, my sounding board, one of my biggest supporters and pushers in everything...was gone. My children's auntie, ice cream and snack pusher, laugh-until-we-cried friend...was gone. Life was different, and I cannot begin to describe the pain. It was one thing for us as adults to experience the loss, but my heart ached for her teenage son. I knew how much she adored him, how she was a pillar for him, and the thought of all this added another layer of pain. This pain was severe because it was abrupt.

Now, all we had were memories. I remember reading our text messages, reviewing pictures, recalling conversations, and aching that we could not create more. I would drive to the grocery store, missing our routine conversation. Her passing changed our lives and I really didn't know where to begin in the healing. We were a safe place for each other; the fire was turned up losing her.

It was approaching her birthday, just a few months after she had left, and this is when I experienced that anxiety attack mentioned in previous chapters. I could not understand; I had faced loss and death before, so I should have been able to process this and heal but the grief was mounting. The timing of when I experienced the episode was a few weeks prior to her birthday and we were planning a celebration in her honor. I never made the correlation to this until I was writing this book. I realized that was a connection and I had not fully processed the grief. I was carrying compounded grief and my body knew it. I was fighting inside, trying to understand this feeling and still this pain.

I realized that in two years, I had lost two very important people in my life. My grandmother had transitioned in 2014 and my best friend and sister in 2016. In addition to this, the family's financial changes brought extreme pressure. It truly seemed like the bottom was falling out of our lives. I thought I had taken good time to grieve, but I now realize that I needed more.

So often we are being strong and should not falter, but it is acceptable to take a pause and breathe. Oftentimes we just keep moving and aren't always taught how to grieve properly, because "life must go on." It must go on, but it is not healthy to just stay on autopilot. There is no award for holding everything in. There is no award for not having a safe place to share. People are looking in from the outside and have no idea of all the processes happening mentally, emotionally, and spiritually. Grief had presented a fight.

I will admit that the loss of my grandmother was hard, but especially at such a "rocky" time in our lives. I wanted to tell her about all of it. My comfort was that I realized she had given me the wisdom that would last and carry me, and I would be able to impart it to others. I was eventually able to accept her leaving.

My sister and best friend's transition was extremely difficult to handle. She was a vital part of my life. She was not just a friend to me, but she was a family member to us. My parents claimed her as their seventh child, and she was extremely proud of that. Her birth mother left before she did but knew the same about my parents and they happily shared a daughter.

There was still so much to do and tell, for she still was young and vibrant.

I decided to continue to make her proud by excelling in what I am purposed to do. As I was sharpening my skillset, I remembered her words to me and her push for me. She was one of the main people that spoke to me about my value and natural abilities. She challenged me to turn my passion and gifts into a business.

I will allow their names to ring out as I walk in purpose because I know I had their full support.

I, like that mother of the 9/11 victim, took years to grieve, even when I didn't realize it.

We must not push aside our time to grieve, for it affects everything.

I am not certain about where you come from, but grief is not something that we talked about much in my community. We were there for each other; it was okay to cry, but those things that could happen after the fact were not talked about.

I would like to share some valuable highlights about grief. I hope that it will help you recognize those that may be there presently.

Some of the physical effects of grief are aches and pains, digestive problems, fatigue, headaches, sore muscles, irritability, and even depression. Although some of the above may have other under-lying issues, they can also be attached to grief.

When something has been in your life or possession for a long time, something of importance and now it's no longer there, we must process it and make necessary adjustments. It is not healthy to ignore the process of grief because it clogs up your humanity, your emotions, your will, and your motivation.

The ITs we discussed in the previous chapters, suppression, rejection, violation, and lack of confidence, are all some form of loss and grief. There is a part of you not operating at optimal ability.

Grief undealt with can cause emotions to spiral out of control, can cause our minds to be clouded, and thoughts to be fragmented. Grief not fully processed will cause an inner fight; grief denied will take you off course.

Grief is not something you can just sleep off; it must be processed. We have to acknowledge and accept the changes in our lives. It is painful and touches our entire pond of life. Each of our processing times will be different. There are moments when you may want to be selfish, don't want to speak or explain yourself or your emotional state to anyone. Whatever length of time it takes you, just don't stop processing and healing. When we avoid processing grief, it can leave the door open for adverse behaviors or thoughts to enter.

Clinically grief is processed in stages and some writers note additional steps, but the basic five are denial, anger, bargaining, depression, and acceptance.

https://grief.com/the-five-stages-of-grief/

Loss of any kind requires the processing of these steps, whether it is human life, animal life, relationship, career, job loss, loss of home, and even a change of status that can feel like a loss.

You may never overcome the loss of a loved one; you simply learn how to cope. Nevertheless, some other losses can cause us to refine and gain power. If you lose a job or a possession, you may be able to refine your skills and create a better version of yourself.

No IT that you face in your life can defeat you, but we must have a willingness to process and keep going. We want to be in a healthy state with ourselves and let go of the things that make us feel heavy. With letting go, we must put strategies in place to keep our peace and put forth the effort to live. You may have to write out your emotions, do some self-talk, and talk with others: holding grief in is not a healthy option. Be aware that grief may cause you to want to disconnect from people, places, and things in your life, but my hope is that you can get professional help, maintain some social interaction, and keep processing.

I am so excited that I faced the challenge to pen this book. Despite every obstacle, I experienced a deeper level of freedom. I am so excited that I left my previous career; I can see the value in it now. When I look at our children and the time we are able to invest in their growth and development, it is irreplaceable. Yes, it comes with great sacrifice, but I can see the benefits. Although the career change was initially hidden grief for me, it was a change that altered my path for greater. I am now pursuing my purpose in a different manner.

1. What is an area that you experienced a major loss?
2. Can you remember how it made you feel?
3. Did you process it?

Chapter 17

OVERCOMING IT

Note to the trusted listening party:

I want to note here- to the ones who may have to hear a story of someone aiming to get over something. It's important to remember that everyone's pain is not processed the same. Everyone's trauma or issue is the worst to them—this is not the time to make comparisons. This is not the time to minimize pain and their view of it. This is the time to be present and listen. There is no cookie-cutter healing. However, everyone will need a safe space when trying to overcome. It's important for the person listening not to be selfish. In order to help someone overcome an obstacle, one must possess empathy. Empathy requires the listener to feel and care, even if there is no ability to personally relate. The one who is listening must allow the victim to speak in honesty and truth about where they are. Listen attentively and thank them for their courage to share their heart and emotions.

If you do not have the capacity to feel and be empathetic, please let the violated know that you don't have it. Anytime someone is brave enough to open up to you about their conflict, they are trusting you with a vulnerable space.

The danger of abruptly telling someone to "get over it" can portray that you don't care: don't care to listen, don't care about their feelings or emotions, and don't care about the pain that was experienced. DO NOT minimize their moment.

Back to the wounded:

Your obstacle, trauma, scenario and process is different from anyone else's. I am asking you to recognize that whatever obstacle appeared in your life brought a weight, but you have the authority to cut all strings and power of that weight. The obstacle-pebble can cause you to halt. When we halt at a particular place in our lives because of circumstances, the experience of trying to move beyond it can be grueling. The thing can and will take from us until we do get over it.

To succeed at getting over anything, we must elevate and climb up so that we are higher than the obstacle. This is my angle in this book, requesting you to elevate beyond what you have experienced. Elevate your actions, your thoughts, and ultimately your life. My goal is never to minimize your pain, trauma, or adversity, but to make you larger than IT. Adversity plays no favorites, we will all face some. We can choose to stay low or rise above it. We can't allow it to defeat us but must maintain a posture of "It didn't defeat me, and I continue to conquer. I will pull myself up and go back to get others, because I remember what it feels like to be weighed down."

It is difficult to swim through life with weights. You have so much purpose and value that you can't afford to sink. Therefore, you must GET OVER IT! It must be said, but with pure motives and the sole intention of seeing you live your best life in your best state. I have told you so many reasons why you can't stay under IT, and my hope is that you believe and see the champion in you.

To overcome, you must make a choice to get up and get over it- whatever your obstacle or issue was. The goal is to not stay under IT, be tormented, nor totally defined by it. IT cannot have the best of you. The ITs come and go, but you have to make an intentional goal to always achieve victory, always win, and always prevail over and through any obstacle. Not by vengeance but from a place of freedom, for you must know what to do when ITs come.

If we can look through a lens that is not jaded, we can find some strength with what we have endured and overcome. Being honest, you didn't like the process, but you gained muscle and have now increased your capacity to hold up someone else because you didn't quit. Undoubtedly, the things that you faced allowed you to learn more about yourself, your strengths and weaknesses, likes, dislikes, and things that you do not want to repeat.

Some painful moments in your life have pushed you through stagnation and given you the motivation to move. Anytime you are faced with something, there is always a choice; to sink or swim, hold on or let go, make a wise choice or a bad one, fight the process or endure and conquer in the process.

So how do we get over IT?

What if anytime there is an unhealthy occurrence in your life, you choose to deal with it immediately and eject it? Would our lives, outlooks, and perspectives be different?

When someone offends you, you let it go or set a healthy boundary and process the situation.

I will not be so insensitive as to ignore that there are degrees of things, pains, and hurts. Someone stepping on your toe is not the same as being held up at gunpoint, or someone punching you in the face. A surface wound will take less time to heal than a gunshot wound, but we can agree that they both can heal. That's the context in which I want you to hear me; they both CAN HEAL. You can heal.

When an occurrence initially takes place in your life, it's still fresh, can be identified, and can be discarded or shelved. We want to choose not to shelf it. When its shelved, you can forget the details of the occurrence and it dully sits in the recesses of your mind or emotions. When you shelf it, you allow a weed to grow and become a root. The longer we allow things to fester in our lives, the blurrier the initial reason becomes, but the secondary effects, symptoms, get stronger. The symptoms cross over into other areas of our lives. The symptoms create a web in which you become a prisoner. It's time to ask the question. Do I really want to allow something to hold me forever?

> **The longer we allow things to fester in our lives, the blurrier the initial reason becomes, but the secondary effects, symptoms, get stronger.**

However, if we quickly address a matter with a calm thought process, we can decide what really happened, get our takeaways/ lessons, and discard the drama and the trash, not allowing it to take up space on the hard drive of our mind. We can keep our emotions healthy, our minds clear, and our thoughts precise by overcoming it.

In the animal kingdom, a spider creates a web. The black widow hangs upside down, as she waits for her prey to enter the web. This pose is to convey the message to predators that she is toxic. The spider hangs upside down; as a human, this would cause great imbalance and a ton of other problems. You would not be able to stay in an upside-down position long without experiencing adverse effects. View being off course, off of the purpose path as hanging upside down. The ITs that brought an interruption, the abuse, violation, and all its neighbors, are a hanging upside down and making it imperative to quickly change your position.

The black widow spider is nearly blind, so she depends on feeling to determine her actions. (www.livescience.com) If a male is interested in mating with her, he must vibrate his abdomen in a certain manner so that she knows what he is aiming to communicate. If he does not and just enter the web, she will eat him. Her venom is 15 times more poisonous than a rattlesnake and this habit keeps her in a cycle of being alone. We don't want to become predatory, lose sight of what is important, and kill off what is to help us create a future. Our emotions are part of life, but we are not to be solely led by them, if we are to make wise decisions and use sound judgment.

It is vitally important for us to heal so that we can see, have visions, dream dreams, and birth greatness as we walk in our purposes.

Overcoming is easier to attain when you let go of offense and pain, remembering how it made you feel and not wanting to inflict it upon anyone else.

Overcoming IT empowers you and allows you to be uninhibited, experiencing true freedom and happiness. The peace that God promises can possess your soul, now that you are over IT.

You must keep PURPOSE, your why—in focus, submerge yourself in it, sharpen and strengthen it so that you can assist others to achieve theirs: all else is a smokescreen. All the pebbles, interruptions and challenges- goal was to get you never to fulfill what God intended. The pebbles in the pond had to land somewhere. Maybe they landed on the floor of your heart as they would on the floor of the pond, what are you going to do with them? Will you leave these life's incidents in your life to keep you heavy or will your just throw them out and act as if nothing occurred, or- build something. Take the pebbles in the pond and build something, build something great out of your adversity. Surely, the pebble was thrown in your pond and may have thrown you off temporarily, but the good news is YOU OWN THE ENTIRE POND.

WORK IT OUT QUESTIONS

In the book, there were questions posed as you read along, and others added. This area is for you to expound and excavate. Prayerfully, these questions will help you to clarify matters and allow you to experience abundant life and peace. Go as far as you need to with your answers.

This tool is not to replace therapy, counseling, or personal interaction. It's to help increase your awareness and healing so that you can live with intention, clarity, and direction.

CHAPTER 1 **You Have Purpose**

What is your purpose?

_____

_____

What makes you happy?

_____

_____

_____

What are you passionate about?

_____

_____

_____

Is there something you would do even if you never got a paycheck for it, and still be fulfilled?

_____

_____

_____

_____

What is on your bucket list?

_____

_____

If you had a dream job, what would it be?

_____

_____

Are any of the above answers pushed to the side?

_____

_____

_____

How did you choose the career that you are currently in or the degree of studies?

_____

_____

Do you have a passion for a certain group of people? (I.e. children, teens, geriatrics, men, women.)

_____

_____

Chapter 2 **IN TIME**

What are your strengths and gift areas?

_____

_____

What have you been dreaming about, visualizing?

_____

_____

What areas do you want to strengthen?

_____

_____

What are some things that currently frustrate you? Can you create a solution? What would the solution look like?

_____

_____

_____

_____

Do you feel limited in a particular area? Please explain.

_____

_____

Have you shrunk or diminished based on something you heard or experienced?

_____

_____

Have you ever been rejected? Explain where and how it made you feel. What can you learn from this "NO"?

_____

_____

Are you an exhorter of potential?

_____

_____

Do you like to help others?

_____

_____

Do you like to host events?

_____

_____

Are you gifted with administration and logistics skills?

_____

_____

What would your life look like without an obstacle?

_____

_____

If money wasn't an object, what would you do for a career?

_____

_____

Where would you attend school? Would you go to college?

_____

_____

What city would you live in?

_____

_____

What are your gift areas that you have identified?

_____

_____

Have you accomplished any part of the goals that you dream about?

_____

_____

_____

_____

Chapter 3 **PURPOSE MUST BE IDENTIFIED**

Who are you?

_____

_____

What do you like to do?

_____

_____

What is your hobby?

_____

_____

Are you growing in life or do you feel like you are in a cycle? What is the cycle?

_____

_____

What are you actively creating?

_____

_____

What new challenges have you accepted?

_____

_____

What are your priorities in life?

_____

_____

Who are you?

_____

_____

What are your current roles?

_____

_____

How would you describe yourself? Use five adjectives.

_____

_____

What kind of people do you attract?

_____

_____

How do you think other people see you?

_____

_____

How can you tell someone else to care for you?

_____

_____

How can you promote a healthy balance in this earth and in your personal world?

_____

_____

If you were to assess the people in your life, can you identify gifts that can be nurtured that will help bring clarity of their existence?

_____

_____

Can you look at the young people in your life and see some of their strengths?

_____

_____

Chapter 4 **WHAT DO YOU POSSESS?**

What has been weighing you down?

_____

_____

Are there any gifts that you have dumbed down to appease others?

_____

_____

What has been your greatest victory in your life?

_____

_____

Do you feel like something was taken from you?

_____

_____

If given 30 seconds tell me three wonderful things about you.

_____

_____

Chapter 5 **THE IT OF TRAUMA**

Can you recall a traumatic event that happened in your life?

_____

_____

Did this event throw you off course?

_____

_____

If yes, what did life look like before this happened?

_____

_____

If yes, what did this event teach you about yourself?

_____

_____

What emotions are associated with this event?

_____

_____

What has been one of the biggest fights in your life?

_____

_____

Can you remember when the fight started?

_____

_____

Have you ever been violated in any manner?

_____

_____

How did you process this violation?

_____

_____

What are some of the secondary effects that you experienced from violation (e.g., attitude, habits, frustrations)?

_____

_____

Do you remember the first time that you recognized fear in your life?

_____

_____

Chapter 6 **YOU WILL MASTER IT**

Do you have great memories of your childhood?

_____

_____

Do you have a healthy relationship with your parents?

_____

_____

What is one of the most memorable moments of your childhood?

_____

_____

Are there any recognizable phobias that you developed from childhood?

_____

_____

Have you dropped something-not finished, prior to mastering the skill?

_____

_____

Can you identify what you dropped?

_____

_____

What is stopping you from returning to it?

_____

_____

Have you ever felt defeated in any area of your life, especially as a child?

_____

_____

Do you recognize that you are a winner?

_____

_____

Please highlights some of your WINS!

_____

_____

Chapter 7 **THE IT OF REJECTION**

Have you ever been rejected?

_____

_____

What are some of your most challenging relationships?

_____

_____

What personality is agitated by your presence?

_____

_____

Do you realize that you are not the only one in the ship? Relationships are a partnership.

What is your idea of a healthy relationship?

_____

_____

Are you happy with yourself? Scale it 1-10, 10 being the highest.

_____

_____

Chapter 8 **SUPPRESSION**

Can you remember a time when you didn't want to share your ideas or dreams?

_____

_____

Have you ever struggled with your creativity?

_____

_____

Do you remember a "NO" that crushed you?

_____

_____

Has anything diminished in your life? Your laughter? Your social life?

_____

_____

Do you feel pressure to perform? From who? Is it healthy?

_____

_____

Can you recall a negative word spoken in your life that may have halted or slowed your flow?

_____

_____

How did you combat the words?

_____

_____

Were you ever told that you weren't successful?

_____

_____

Have you ever felt like a failure?

_____

_____

Were you often compared with others in your family?

_____

_____

Did you have a teacher or mentor that taunted your dreams?

_____

_____

Did you believe them?

_____

_____

Chapter 9 **WHEN IT MAKES YOU MUTE**

Do you remember a time when you could not put your feelings into words?

_____

_____

Can you identify where this originated?

_____

_____

Can you recall a scenario that made you feel vulnerable?

_____

_____

Have you ever wanted to quit?

_____

_____

Have you ever felt like a failure?

_____

_____

Chapter 10 **THE STRUGGLE AFTER THE WOUND**

In what areas have you been wounded?

_____

_____

Did you put up a wall with others after being wounded?

_____

_____

Do you struggle with the idea of trusting others?

_____

_____

What did distrust keep you from?

_____

_____

Are you willing to stay in the wounded space indefinitely?

_____

_____

What is an area in your life that makes you angry or causes irritability?

_____

_____

Have you identified relationships that have caused you pain?

_____

_____

How did you let go of those relationships, via avoidance or attempting peaceful resolve?

_____

_____

Have you forgiven those that hurt you?

_____

_____

Have you forgiven yourself for hurting others?

_____

_____

Have you recognized the entry point in your life that made you apprehensive about love?

_____

_____

How will you wash your wound, cleanse your heart? (What healthy behavior do you practice?)

_____

_____

What healthy intentional actions will you take to be free in spirit?

_____

_____

What treatment plan will you put in place? How often will you implement healthy healing activities?

_____

_____

Chapter 11 **WHAT'S SAID CAN HELP TO FRAME YOU**

What positive affirmations and self-talk are you speaking to frame your world with your words?

_____

_____

Create a daily plan of affirmation using the ABC format. Insert I am/I will/I am becoming/I believe/I have ... (i.e., A - a positive attitude. B - Boldness. C - Courage, etc.).

_____

_____

Chapter 12 **WHEN IT CAUSES YOU TO FIGHT**

What is one of the areas in which you have had to fight?

_____

_____

What are some labels that you realize are lies, but they caused you to fight? They have no power over you.

_____

_____

Chapter 13 **THE IT OF VIOLATION**

Is there an area in your life in which you have been violated?

_____

_____

If yes, have you confronted it?

_____

_____

What did you do with that experience?

_____

_____

Have you ever been intentionally overlooked?

_____

_____

Chapter 14 **WHEN IT CAUSES YOU TO FEAR**

Are you living beneath your abilities?

_____

_____

Are you living above your means?

_____

_____

Are you seeking validation from others? If so, WHO?

_____

_____

Did you have an experience that stopped you in your tracks?

_____

_____

Chapter 15 **WHEN IT CAUSES YOU TO LOSE CONFIDENCE**

What is your vision?

_____

_____

Use three adjectives for your personality.

_____

_____

What do you want others to see in you and say about you?

_____

_____

Chapter 16 **THE IT OF GRIEF**

Name a major area in which you have experienced loss.

_____

_____

What is an area in which you experienced hardship?

_____

_____

How did you respond to either?

_____

_____

What do you do to relieve stress?

_____

_____

Chapter 17 **OVERCOMING IT**

What have you recognized about yourself while reading this book?

_____

_____

Have you made progress?

_____

_____

What holes have you closed?

_____

_____

What are your strengths?

_____

_____

REFERENCES

"Purpose." Merriam-Webster. Merriam-Webster. Accessed September 26, 2019. https://www.merriam-webster.com/dictionary/purpose.

"Trauma." Trauma / SAMHSA-HRSA. Accessed September 26, 2019. https://www.integration.samhsa.gov/clinical-practice/trauma.

"Did You Know...You Have Between 50,000 And 70,000 Thoughts ..." Accessed October 11, 2019. https://www.huffington-post.co.uk/shahilla-barok/did-you-knowyou-have-be-tw_b_11819532.html.grief.com. Accessed October 12, 2019. https://grief.com/the-five-stages-of-grief/.

"Male Spiders Must Twerk - or Be Eaten." LiveScience. Purch. Accessed January 12, 2020. https://www.livescience.com/42653-spider-mating-twerking.html.

"Black Widow Spider Facts." LiveScience. Purch. Accessed January 12, 2020. https://www.livescience.com/amp/39919-black-widow-spiders.html.

"Sticks and stones may break my bones, but WORDS NEVER HURT!" author unknown?

CPSIA information can be obtained
at www.ICGtesting.com
Printed in the USA
LVHW011925280620
659167LV00012B/579

9 781630 505882